FOR
A
DEEPER
LIFE

FOR A DEEPER LIFE

GRACE S. DAWSON

Abingdon Press • New York • Nashville

FOR A DEEPER LIFE

Copyright © 1963 by Abingdon Press

Library of Congress Catalog Card Number: 63-8667

Scripture quotations as designated are from the Revised
Standard Version of the Bible, copyrighted 1946 and
1952 by the Division of Christian Education, National
Council of the Churches, and are used by permission.

SET UP, PRINTED, AND BOUND BY THE
PARTHENON PRESS, AT NASHVILLE,
TENNESSEE, UNITED STATES OF AMERICA

*To all my
friends of the Spirit
everywhere*

FOREWORD

This small volume is intended to be an introduction and an invitation to a deeper way of life, the way of prayer. It is hoped that it may interest the reader in making a serious study of the life of prayer through one of the more comprehensive books on the subject. Also it is thought that this book may help a leader in preparing devotional material according to topic.

I want to thank Howard Clinebell, associate professor of pastoral counseling at Southern California School of Theology, who read chap. 23. Thanks are due also to the authors and publishers who have granted me permission to quote from their works in connection with various chapters.

For permission to include poems in the text of certain chapters, I wish to express grateful appreciation to the following contemporary poets: Katherine Edelman, Elinor Lennen, Clara Aiken Speer, Velma West Sykes, Dorothy Brown Thompson, and May Williams Ward.

GRACE S. DAWSON

CONTENTS

9

WHEN SHADOWS COME

THE WIDER VIEW

SEEKING
AND
FINDING

1. *The Inner Life*

Keep thy heart with all diligence; for out of it
are the issues of life.   Prov. 4:23

Little as some people realize it, we are living two
lives. There is an outer life, the life observed by our
families, our neighbors, and friends—the life of going
and doing and talking. This outer life is demanding;
it presses upon us with its hurry and clamor. Owing
to ease of travel we cover much distance. Owing to
ease of communication we admit many voices, many
requests.

But there is also an inner life, where we are alone—
the life of thinking and feeling. It is this life which is
likely to be overlooked in the rush and thrust of our
outer lives with the heavy demands on our time and
attention. It is the inner life which is too often
squeezed into the narrow compass between activities,
fed on scraps, starved until it becomes thin and
withered.

The two lives are essential to each other. It takes

11

both of them to make a full experience, a life of growth and maturity. They should intermesh and react upon each other. In our present existence the inner life is the one most likely to be neglected.

We need to discover our own souls. We need to look under the ready-made opinions and attitudes garnered from outer sources and find out what we actually think and feel. For this inner life is where we plant our roots as individuals, where we become real people. This is the life of the soul, the place where we seek and find God, the garden of spiritual growth.

What do we mean by seeking and finding God within? I think it means the recognition that here within we are related to the infinite creative Power which brought us with all creation into being. In every creative act something of the creator gets into the thing created. This is true of the painter, the composer, the poet—into each of his works the artist puts a very real part of himself, which has an influence wherever the work of art is appreciated. This is a parable God has given us—a parable of his own creativity. Into each part of his creation he put something of his own creative power. On every level of his ladder of evolution we can see this creative power at work, building, creating, reaching upward toward a higher development, until it attains the height of intelligence in humanity.

Thus there is some part deep within each of us of that divine Power, God himself astir within. When we recognize this and begin to attend to it, our lives are changed, broadened, deepened. God will not urge or compel. He invites us by his presence to a greater understanding of life and a fuller knowledge of ourselves. He would expand our horizons and enlarge our capacities for living.

Most of us have felt at some time the need to deepen life. We should like to find and hold fast to something more than the busy round of daily living. We need to find meaning and purpose in life and a clean sense of values. These are treasures of the inner life. They are gifts of God and are not to be had merely for the wishing. They must be sought. God must be sought. He is the source of the richer, deeper life, and he waits within.

This deepening takes time—time and earnestness in the search, time to be alone and quiet, time to think. Difficult? Of course it is difficult, like most worthwhile things. Everything conspires to absorb the time and intrude upon the quiet. But little by little, with persistence, it can be managed. One can get up a little earlier or go to bed a little later, set aside some less essential thing, use a space of minutes between necessary duties. For this is necessary, too, for footage in reality. Christ knew the necessity for deep rootage. Remember the good seed that sprang up too quickly and "because it had no root it withered away" (Mark 4:5-6).

The first test of the desire for deepening is the ability to find time for God. If something else must be cut short or omitted, that is to be accepted. Life is made up of choices, and here begins a lesson in the examination of values. The choice is a first step.

Send my roots deeper, Lord, more deep in life,
    Below the pang of failure, brief success,
Below the desperate haste, the unslaked thirst
    For hearts that understand and hands that bless.
Send my roots deeper, Lord, more deep in truth,
    Below the facile murmurs that applaud,
Surly ill will, indifferent circumstance,
    To the eternal treasuries of God.
Send my roots deeper, Lord, more deep in love,
    Below glib protestations to the springs
Of humble service given joyously,
    The largess of the small unnoticed things.
Send my roots deeper, Lord, more deep in thee,
That I stand steadfast, growing tall and free.[1]

2. *Attention Is the Door*

> Behold, I stand at the door, and knock: if any man
> hear my voice, and open the door, I will come in
> to him, and will sup with him, and he with me.
> REV. 3:20

Making time for the inner life is the first step,
but the important thing is to receive God into that
life. He is waiting; he is ready to come in, but if we
would have him as our guest we must open the door.
The door is *attention*. To receive God means to give
him complete attention, to make him real to ourselves.

[1] Grace S. Dawson, "Send My Roots Deeper."

14

That which is real only becomes real to us as we give our attention to it. There is a lovely flower in this room, but unless we stop and quietly observe it, unless we carefully look at it, smell and enjoy it, it is not real to us, and we are unable to gather in its beauty. It only becomes real to us, it is only *realized,* when we turn our attention onto it.[1]

To *realize* God's presence means to achieve a constant awareness of his nearness. Start the day with a little space of minutes given to this. One excellent way to begin is to read a short passage from the Bible or from some good devotional book. Then pause and think about what you have read, lifting your thoughts in a momentary prayer for understanding. Is there a meaning here for you? Look for a special bit to take with you through the day, a "spiritual nosegay" this has been called. Then quiet your mind for a minute or two and just be still before God, awaiting his blessing. Such a brief period of meditation and devotion is important in building up a sense of the presence of God, an awareness of his presence as a great reality.

The inner life can be lived in the presence of God as it is lived in the possession of a great human love. Such a love as this becomes the background of all thinking, a steadying force, a light that shines through every experience. There is no effort necessary to turn the thoughts toward the loved one. They turn there of themselves.

Consider the greatness and the love of God until

[1] Clarence Neff in *The New Life News.* Used by permission.

it becomes a part of you. Form the habit of lifting the heart in some single phrase, "Love to thee, Lord!" A prayer such as this is called a "prayer of aspiration," or sometimes, a "flash prayer." Make God a part of every task, of every joy. Live the day with him. This is awareness, and this is what brings richness and depth into life. Living becomes significant, full of meaning.

Look for God in all aspects of the world around you. You may not be able to walk in the woods or follow a mountain trail. But for everyone there is the morning sunshine at the window, the call of a bird, the friendly greeting of a neighbor, the daily, faithful comradeship of a fellow worker. These can be God's messengers to you if you respond. Here is the presence of God, his signature of beauty on the day.

Living with the thought of God brings meaning into life. It adds spaciousness; tensions tend to relax and fretting to vanish. Breathe in God with the very air and with thanks. "Glory to God!" The minutes between appointments or the ride home from work can bring quiet and a lifting of mood. Keep the inner life in God's peace and the outer life will lose its power to absorb and disturb.

This world is full of its Creator—his life, his power, his marvelous touch of beauty and perfection. Too bad that most of us have grown up losing the child's gift of wonder! Let's find it again—the quick spontaneous response to the beauty of little things, the smile of recognition in the eyes of a friend, the care-

16

free whistle of a passing boy, the joy of watching clouds racing in the wind. So many of us are blind much of the time. God's world is full of him and we give it little of ourselves. *Attention is the doorway,* and if we can learn to open it a little wider now and then, much of beauty and wonder can come in.

Thou dost pervade thy world! Each nodding flower
   With intricate design spells out thy skill;
Free wind and wave portray the rhythmic power
   Which lifts and looses ever at thy will.
Thou art beyond the stars, profound, immense,
   Yet livest in the very grass below,
Speakest within the ocean's turbulence
   And in the gentle quiet of the snow.
In friendship, man to man, thou hast a part,
   And in the sturdy good of common things.
Thou art in all! And wheresoe'er thou art
   Beauty appears and truth her challenge flings.
Still thou dost let me find thee in my heart!
   Still thou dost bless me 'til the spirit sings.[2]

3. *The Preparation*

God is love; he who dwells in love is dwelling
in God, and God in him.
           I JOHN 4:16 N.E.B.

When I think what it means to live in daily companionship with God, I find myself taking a

[2] Grace S. Dawson, "Immanence."

17

good look at my life. Is it a fit place for God's dwelling? Facing the situation is like turning a strong light upon myself. Things appear different in that light, and there is much that I know must be changed to provide a setting for this wonderful companionship. My personality needs a real housecleaning.

"He who dwells in love is dwelling in God, and God in him." Can all the areas of my life stand this test of love? How can I make it fit for the dwelling place of my Lord?

> Be gladly busy, Soul, today—
> A royal Guest comes down the way.
> Make ready for his welcoming—
> Remove each soiled or tarnished thing.
> Then make all fair and clean within
> Where dark and dustiness have been.
> Sweep every room, swing windows wide
> To let the sunshine stream inside.
> And if the light reveal some stain
> That spite of effort shall remain,
> Grieve not—if you have done your best
> His gracious touch will cleanse the rest.
> Be joyous, Soul, put doubt away,
> Invite him in and bid him stay.[1]

No matter how sincerely we have tried to lead a good life, there are things incompatible with God's very presence. There may be resentment or an old grudge half-forgotten. There may be a little jealousy of someone or the coveting of something we think

[1] Grace S. Dawson, "Royal Guest."

18

should be ours. There are pet prejudices, perhaps, or little streaks of narrowness often interfering with sound judgment. We all have something to reckon with. This is a demanding situation, and we have to face some changes in our way of thinking and living.

But God himself is not hard or demanding. He knows these human hearts which he has created. He will take us as we are. All he wants is the sincere *desire* to change, to let his gracious Spirit enter and take over. Then changes will begin to come. Perhaps right here we should speak of the different ways we may think of this companionship with the divine. The same experience comes to different people according to these different ways.

A story is told of a waggish college student who thought to put a poser to his minister father, "Give me some advice, Dad," he said. "Which shall I seek, the Father, the Son, or the Holy Spirit?"

"My son," replied the older man promptly, "if you get a good hold on any one of the three I shall have no worry about you."

To some people the divine companionship means the overshadowing love of the Creator God, our Father in heaven, to whom Jesus prayed. Others think of themselves as walking and talking with the human Jesus, in the warm relationship enjoyed by his disciples. A friend of mine, describing her feeling in a certain trying situation, said, "I just put my hand into the hand of Jesus." To others the experience is being filled with a strength and beauty which could only be that of the Holy Spirit, the

"Counselor" whom Jesus promised to send to his followers.

But it is the same God who made us and loves us, who walked the earth in Jesus of Nazareth as the Christ, and who fills our hearts with his Spirit when we seek his fellowship. Most of us realize this, and we find God at various times under different images. For God himself overflows all the words that can be used to describe him, exceeds all the pictures we can make of him. He includes and goes beyond our human imaginations and gives himself to us under whatever name we seek him.

Whatever the picture by which we make him real to ourselves, God is ready and eager to come and live with us. Of course our lives are not spotless, even if we have been good citizens and active church members for years. It needs our real surrender, his constant nearness, his hand upon us to rid us of self-centered attitudes and petty faults. He must take us as we are and make us what he would have us be. This he will do if we let him, if we open the door and invite him into our daily living.

Our gracious God, we marvel at thy greatness and glory and the goodness which responds to our need. Humbly we acknowledge our unworthiness. Come into our lives and make them beautiful with thy love and light. Take all we have and are, and use it for our growth and to thy glory. In Jesus' name and for his sake. AMEN.

4. *A Rosary of Song*

Bless the Lord, O my soul: and all that is
within me, bless his holy name.

Ps. 103:1

This is a very personal chapter. It goes back to
the early days of my own adventuring into the divine
fellowship. God is always with us, but we are not
always with him. In order to keep myself in the
presence of God, I needed help in directing my
thoughts and feelings. Such help I found in singing.
Many people, as I, even without good voices, sing at
their work. It *can* be done almost under the breath.

Everyone has had experience with the tune which
he "cannot get out of his head," and which stays
there all day long, recurring after it was thought forgotten. If the air is monotonous and the words are
silly this can be an annoying experience. But if the
song is chosen for the definite effect it has on the
spirit, this tendency of a tune to haunt the singer
can be turned to account. The song becomes a friend.
Without being summoned it brings back again and
again throughout the day a mood which consoles or
uplifts. It is like a gentle hand laid on the shoulder,
reminding, comforting, blessing.

Certain songs of personal counsel have come to
mean much to me; they have become an affirmation
which reassures me of God's presence and keeps me
in tune with life. "Count Your Blessings" is a good
old-fashioned remedy for the blues:

Are you ever burdened with a load of care?
Does the cross seem heavy you are called to bear?

21

Count your many blessings, every doubt will fly,
And you will be singing as the days go by.
Count your blessings, name them one by one:
Count your blessings, See what God hath done.

EDWIN O. EXCELL

There are other hymns with beautiful words on which to ponder. We should remember that a hymn is seldom made to order. The words are born out of someone's heart experience, and carry real meaning for other hearts. Some seem to be meant especially for me.

Spirit of God, descend upon my heart;
    Wean it from earth; through all its pulses move;
Stoop to my weakness, mighty as Thou art,
    And make me love Thee as I ought to love.

· · · · · · · · · · · · · ·

Teach me to love Thee as Thine angels love,
    One holy passion filling all my frame;
The kindling of the heaven-descended dove,
    My heart an altar and Thy love the flame.

GEORGE CROLY

Most beautiful of all and most completely my own is a certain lovely aria from *Elijah* by Mendelssohn, based on the thirty-seventh psalm.

O rest in the Lord, wait patiently for Him,
And He shall give thee thy heart's desires;
O rest in the Lord, wait patiently for Him,

22

And He shall give thee thy heart's desires.
And He shall give thee thy heart's desires.
Commit thy way unto Him, and trust in Him;
Commit thy way unto Him, and trust in Him;
And fret not thyself because of evildoers.
O rest in the Lord, wait patiently for Him,
Wait patiently for Him;
O rest in the Lord, wait patiently for Him,
And He shall give thee thy heart's desires,
O rest in the Lord, wait patiently for Him,
And He shall give thee thy heart's desires,
And He shall give thee thy heart's desires.
O rest in the Lord, O rest in the Lord,
And wait, wait patiently for Him.

Those who know the music will understand why
I cannot leave out any of the lines despite the repeti-
tion. When discouragement or impatience threatens
my serenity or some particular barrier raises itself,
I literally sing it away. Sometimes I spend a whole
day with one song and never tire of it. I have come
to realize that in this manner God can take away
an unworthy desire and give my heart a more worthy
one, and this has become my fervent prayer.

Thus I have made up my "rosary of song," choosing for each occasion the song which best suits the
particular need from those which I have found and
loved. For people who do not sing at all, the recalling
of poems can have much the same effect. I heard a
minister suggest studying the hymnbook as a collec-
tion of spiritual experience. And many psalms are
wonderful memory treasures.

Our Father, we thank thee for musicians and poets who have given expression to the longings of our hearts. Bless our attempts to keep ourselves close to thee. Give us a living song in our hearts that our lives may make music for thee through our devotion. AMEN.

5. *Our Daily Bread*

He told them another parable. "The Kingdom of heaven is like leaven which a woman took and hid in three measures of meal, till it was all leavened." MATT. 13:33 R.S.V.

We do not have any further explanation of this parable. One interpretation is usually accepted. The leaven is the "kingdom of heaven" in the hearts of the followers of Jesus and their witness to the communities around them. This witness makes the Kingdom grow until the whole world shall be brought into a brotherhood under the loving rule of God.

But there is a closer and more intimate interpretation, which really precedes the explanation above. The kingdom of heaven is like leaven which I must hide in my heart until it grows to fill my whole life. The teaching of Jesus, his often repeated assertion that love is the important thing, must be taken into my consciousness in earnest. I must dwell on it and live with it until it becomes part of the very tissue of my life. It will then affect every area of my actions. It will pervade my every attitude and reveal itself in

24

all I say and do. My whole life will be an illustration of the way of love which is the kingdom of heaven.

There was another occasion on which Jesus used the idea of leaven to teach a lesson. Jesus and his disciples had set out on a short journey, and the men had forgotten to bring any bread with them. Jesus said to them, "Take heed and beware of the leaven of the Pharisees and of the Sadducees." This really upset the disciples, and caused them to argue with one another about his meaning. Some no doubt thought that he was warning them not to buy the wrong kind of bread.

"Why are you talking this way? You have little faith," said Jesus. "Why do you feel that the question of bread is so important? Don't you remember the five loaves and the many baskets of scraps you gathered up? I was not talking of bread. Beware of the leaven of the Pharisees and Sadducees." Then they understood that he was telling them to beware, not of the leaven which is in bread, but of the *teachings* of the Pharisees and Sadducees. (See Matt. 16:6-12.)

William Barclay in his "Daily Study Bible Series" has an explanation of these teachings.

The Pharisees saw religion in terms of laws and commandments and rules and regulations. . . . of outward ritual and outward purity. . . . This is a warning against a religion of outward respectability, which looks on a man's outward actions and forgets the inner state of his heart.

The Sadducees had two characteristics, which are

25

closely connected. They were wealthy and aristocratic, and they were deeply involved in politics. . . . This may well be a warning against giving material things too high a place in our scheme of values, and against thinking that man can be reformed by political actions.[1]

This warning of Jesus goes right to the root of daily living. What is the food we are giving our hearts and minds day by day? On what does our thinking dwell? Is it material comfort, the accumulation of things? Is it presenting a good appearance, a pious face to the world? Or is it the sincere service of the Kingdom and the love of our fellowmen?

Where do we choose the friends we admire and wish to emulate? From the best-dressed, the socially elite, the affluent and influential? Or from the radiant spirits whose lives speak of God? What are the books we read? Those which merely entertain, or those which inspire, uplift, and stimulate?

The choice is ours. If we would have the companionship of God we must build an atmosphere in our lives in which God can dwell. We must choose the leaven of the kingdom of heaven, the daily bread which truly satisfies, and which can make us grow up to be mature persons—the children of God.

This is no limited choice. The world is his and he made it. It is a question of opening our lives so fully to the light that we come into a new fullness of living, in which spiritual values take precedence over ma-

[1] From *The Gospel of Matthew, II,* 145-46, by William Barclay. Published 1959, The Westminster Press. Used by permission.

terial values. Then the beauty and wealth which he has given are seen in true perspective, and all that we are and have can be used to enlarge our lives and to help and inspire those around us.

Give us, O God, the food we need:
  The clean, sound truth that we should know,
The warm, kind love in word and deed
  By which our human souls will grow.
Give us a faith for every day,
  A firm, high faith, that, amply fed,
We may feed others on our way—
  Give us this day our daily bread.[2]

6. *Friends of the Spirit*

Fulfil ye my joy, that ye be likeminded, having the same love, being of one accord, of one mind.
PHIL. 2:2

One of the loveliest gifts of God to man is friendship. Our hearts naturally seek companionship; that is the way God made us. We are born having relatives. Sometimes we find them sympathetic and congenial, unfortunately sometimes not. On the contrary we *choose* our friends, people we like, whose companionship gives us pleasure and relaxation. But even these friendships are casual, many of them, based on association in the activities of work or play or on some common taste.

[2] Grace S. Dawson, "Our Daily Bread."

Standing out from among our friends in a special light are those whose tie with us goes down to the deeper aspects of life. They are the ones whose souls speak to us, with whom we have the common hopes and ideals of the quest for spiritual things. These are the friends with whom we share a little of the inner life, those whose comradeship feeds us with special nourishment, whose search for beauty and truth answers our own. These are the "friends of the spirit," and there is nothing more precious among our possessions. For this friendship has in it an eternal element, something of the love of God himself.

> Your words vibrate upon my ears,
> Your eyes are mirrors for my own.
> Despair or confidence or fears
> Are shared, not felt alone.
> Because we have a joint concern
> And braid our strength into one strand,
> Time is a school in which we learn
> What secret resource we command,
> How the forbidding seas divide,
> And clouds break that were dark and thick,
> When one-plus-one is multiplied
> In friendship's strange arithmetic.[1]

Happy are those whose lives are enriched by one or more of these deeper attachments. They are not acquired by determination. Sometimes they grow. Sometimes they begin, it seems, almost by chance, when something reveals the bond which lies hidden

[1] Elinor Lennen, "Friend to Friend." Used by permission.

below. But one can prepare the way for such relationships and cherish them.

One way to prepare is to cultivate an attitude of expectation. Remember to keep aware of each person you meet as a *real person,* a soul with a hidden life which may hold treasure to share. Give of yourself, more than superficial answer to question, being ready to respond when the door is open. Don't be timid about speaking of your ideals, quietly, only a word or two when occasion offers. You will be surprised how often there is an answering flash from the inner self of another, where just below the surface there is a desire for understanding.

This is what Martin Buber is saying when he pleads with us for an I-Thou relationship with others. It is what Albert Day is stressing in his book *Dialogue and Destiny.* A true dialogue is a meeting between two selves on the deeper and more genuine level.

There are those who are fortunate enough to belong to a group whose minds are in tune, and whose personalities complement one another. It may be that this is a prayer group, knit by definite spiritual quest into sympathy and affection. It may be, on the other hand, that there is no group bound together in activity, but simply that with this one and that one there is an empathy which goes to the deeper levels.

With such "friends of the spirit" there is a sharing far beyond actual conversation. A spoken sentence will bring a meeting of glances, a nod or a smile which speaks of a depth of understanding. An hour spent with such a friend brings true refreshment, the feeding of the soul which means growth. For there are twice the joys when each is shared, and joy is lifting. There is a great easing of trouble when someone understands to the depth what it means, and new courage for living it through. Over and beyond the comfort of the moment is the infilling of a knowledge of the other, an appreciation of growth on the part of both, a growth made possible by a relationship blessed by God himself.

Our beloved God, who art the very meaning of love, we thank thee for deep friendship, rooted in eternal things. Help us to be worthy of such friendships. AMEN.

7. *The Written Word*

Teach me thy way, O Lord, and lead me
in a plain path.   Ps. 27:11

Not only are we blest with friends of the spirit who share our lives, but there is a whole realm of friends waiting to help us between the covers of books. In the days of the early Christians there were few books, for books were made by hand and were possessed only by the wealthy or by the great libraries. This is one reason why Paul's letters were cherished so carefully, copied and recopied and circulated from group to group.

Today we have ready at hand the testimony of many generations of those who sought and found

God and discovered his strength for their lives. There is truly a book for every taste and every need, another friend of the spirit to guide, teach, and reassure.

We think first of all of the Bible, but here many of us need help. The archaic language of the King James Version is a stumbling block; sometimes it slows us down and blurs the meaning. On the other hand the passages which are most familiar and best loved lose much of their impact because of that very familiarity. We need to see them afresh. Try one of the many excellent new translations, and discover what interesting and often arresting interpretations they offer. There are also fine commentaries which point up new insights. There is nothing better than the study of the Gospels in *The Interpreter's Bible*. Another excellent help is the "Daily Study Bible Series" by William Barclay. Ask God's guidance in choosing Bible help and in following out any study.

It is my personal feeling that everyone who is seeking the depths and heights of spiritual living should, aside from the Bible, keep two books by him, one for instruction and one for inspiration. The difference lies partly in their purpose, partly in their use.

There is so much to learn that it is well to do a little serious reading on the life of prayer. There are many excellent books on the subject. Two I consider especially fine are *Reality and Prayer* by John Magee and *Making Prayer Real* by Lynn J. Radcliffe. Both of these make the unfolding way of prayer clear and help you to enter a new world guided by someone who has walked this way before you.

Through ink upon a printed page
  A living presence takes my hand
And leads me on a pilgrimage
  Into a strange, far-reaching land.

Thought answers thought, and turns the gaze
  Horizon-wide and zenith high,
And I am treading unknown ways
  With new stars burning in the sky.[1]

For inspirational reading, a few pages night or morning to find a thought for the day, a special kind of book is needed. There are books of short readings or meditations, easy to pick up briefly, such as *Letters of the Scattered Brotherhood,* edited by Mary Strong. Or try one of the collections of letters written by a wise spiritual director to a young friend or counselee. Such letters seem to meet your need almost as if written to you personally. One book of this kind is *Letters of Direction* by Abbe de Tourville. Many people find a great deal of help in books of prayers, such as *Prayers for Daily Use* by Samuel Miller. These books and a few others I have listed merely as suggestions in an Appendix. Any good bookstore will order books for you if they are not on hand.

Some people keep a notebook in which to paste or copy inspiring bits from newspapers or magazines. For when we put ourselves in God's care he speaks to us in numerous ways. The word may come through people or books, through sermons, or through the most ordinary events. Everything is his, and can be

[1] Grace S. Dawson, "Communication."

made his messenger to the listening heart. The thing we need to do is learn to listen, so that wherever we are we are never out of touch with his love, his wisdom, his guidance.

If you like to underline your books you will discover another thing. God's messages reach us in unexpected ways and at different times. Try using a pencil of another color for underlining each time you reread a book. You will be surprised at the sentences you missed which now stand out with meaning. Perhaps God has a new word for you. Or perhaps you have just grown a little in the meantime.

Dear Lord of truth, forgive us for our indifference, and awaken us to thy speaking, however it may come. Guide us to the book friends which will help us most, and speak to us through every page. AMEN.

8. *Learning to Listen*

Speak, Lord; for thy servant heareth.
I SAM. 3:9

Living in the presence of God, we learn to listen to him as to a beloved friend. We find him blessing us with a deeper knowledge of the people around us. Sharing with him all our associations and activities, slowly we grow in understanding.

The secret of dwelling within the divine companionship is obedience to the divine will. Jesus made this very clear: "If you keep my commandments, you will

33

abide in my love, just as I have kept my Father's commandments and abide in his love" (John 15:10 R.S.V.).

But how can we be sure of knowing God's will, so that we may be obedient to it? The Jews had a long and complicated code of ritual law to which they felt bound to be obedient. For us this is not true. For us the law has been summed up by Jesus himself, "This is my commandment, that you love one another as I have loved you" (John 15:12 R.S.V.).

To love as Jesus loved! That is indeed a shining ideal to which to direct the gaze. It surely means pushing aside any thought of self. It means the outward-going love that never hesitates to give time, energy, and thought to another who needs help.

But often there is difficulty in knowing just what is the right thing to do. Our lives are very full, and loves and loyalties and interests interfere and sometimes conflict with one another. How can we be sure to choose the right course of action?

The answer is *by listening*. We subdue our own wishes and wait during the creative silence of our prayer hour. Deep in the inner quiet the answers may be formed in our mind. But it is still more important to form the habit of listening to that inner prompting throughout the day. We need to keep ourselves attuned to the guidance which comes when we need it. God speaks to us in many ways, but he cannot get his message across to us if we are not ready to receive it.

He may speak through a sermon or address. I have sat in an audience and heard one sentence spoken as if directly to me. God was sending his word through the speaker's voice. He may speak through a conversation with others or through a book I am reading. There are countless ways for God to make known his will if I have cultivated the habit of being alert to his communication.

God speaks to us often through events. Listening means keeping oneself alert to the changes in outward circumstance. What does God want me to learn from this which has happened to me? Some teachers of prayer believe that if we persist in the dedicated life we shall reach the place where "there is neither chance nor accident." Whether it is an unexpected happiness which comes my way, an opportunity for service perhaps, or something difficult for which I need all my courage and endurance, God is using it to tell me something. What am I to learn from this situation?

We pray that our loved ones will be given strength and growth and fullness of life. Then we grieve if they must go through trials or carry heavy burdens. Listening to God we would surely understand that this is the way of growth, that spiritual muscles must be disciplined. Life has often been called a school, but we forget sometimes that this means lessons are to be learned from the divine Teacher.

When we have learned to listen we go through our days with less tension, facing what comes with confidence. Keeping the commandment of love takes all our time and much of our attention, yet it can be a light burden, carried with rejoicing.

Still the time may come when there is a difficult decision to make, and we listen in vain for God's guidance. We test the situation by all our rules of love. Perhaps there is a conflict here between two demands on us, so that the alternatives seem evenly balanced. We seek advice from those who are wise in the ways of God. We weigh this counsel, listening, and we are still in doubt. What then can we do?

One great teacher's advice is this: Choose according to the best of your values the way you will go, and put the result in God's hand. Then go forward, still listening, asking God to guide every turn of the road. Trust God that your choice may be used for him, and he will bless it and turn it to his glory.

> That I may do my part,
> That I may never miss
> Thy voice that comes to chide,
> To comfort or to guide,
> Lord, give me only this—
> A listening heart.[1]

---

[1] Grace S. Dawson, "Listening Heart."

WALKING
IN THE
LIGHT

9. *Thinking About God*

God is light, and in him is no darkness at all.
I JOHN 1:5

When we try to think about God we realize that words do not help us much. We can do better with pictures. Language begins and grows by means of metaphor, or symbol, describing one thing by likening it to another, something we can see or feel. From the Bible itself we have light as a symbol of God, the most beautiful of all.

Think of God as light. Consider the life-giving sunlight, how it stirs the sleeping seed beneath the sod, unfolds the leaves from tight bud cases, unfurls the velvet spiral of the rose. God has set his sun in the heavens that we may know his great power and glory. Close your eyes and imagine the warm sunlight pouring over you. Don't be afraid to use the imagination; it is the *image-making* power, God's creative gift to us. Use it to help you draw near to God. Imagine his light pouring into you, flooding your soul with a spiritual light. See life through this light, the light of God.

"God is light." What a wonderful parable for the soul! Light means understanding. When you cannot "see" what to do next, when your course of action is in doubt, turn toward the light of God. Be quiet within and try to dismiss all worry, as you allow the light to permeate your mind. Wait for the light, and trust it.

There are other consequences of coming to the light. We see things differently—our values change. Some things we have cherished we find to be unworthy, and we put them aside. It is as though we drew very near a dazzling fire which burned away certain elements of our life. And those who have lived long in the light have about them a radiance. One knows them for dwellers in the light.

Then it begins to dawn upon us that the light may change us also, and we long for such a change. We begin to be willing to have some of our selfishness and willfulness burned away. Perhaps if we drew closer, remained in the light, there might come a transformation in our very self, the self we have come to know as the inner life. Some of that radiance might shine out through our life into the lives of others. What a wonderful thing that would be! Dare we pray for it?

We think of the early Egyptians as idol-worshipers. The greatest of their gods was the sun, most often called Re. Their great pyramids and temples were built with a door set so that the first rays of the rising sun would enter. We are told that their wise men and one of their greatest rulers believed in a supreme God who ruled the world and all its peoples, who was an invisible Spirit, and that the sun was the symbol for his greatness. That was a long time ago, but it is not hard to understand such symbolism. Surely God has always known that little human minds need pictures in order to comprehend his power and his nearness.

Light is life-giving, warmth-bringing, power-building. All these things which sunlight does for the world, God does for the soul as spiritual light. He enlightens our understanding, clarifies that which is confused, and enables us to see things in their right proportions and relationships. A quiet period of musing and meditation, lifted into the light of the Spirit, brings a new and restful attitude. A heavy task brought into the light by a weary worker is performed with increased energy and patient endurance.

When Christ came to live among men, this light came into the world in a new and different way. "In him was life; and the life was the light of men." The world has not been the same since. A great transformation has been going on, because the light is at work in the hearts of men. Unrecognized, the light has penetrated to far countries everywhere. To be sure there is need for further transformation. But "the light shines in the darkness, and the darkness has not overcome it" (John 1:5 R.S.V.).

Burn, holy Light! In beauty calm and clear,
Dispelling doubt, bewilderment, and fear,
Make plain the path before my clouded sight.
Burn, holy Light! Burn on, thou living Light!

Burn, holy Flame! Consume each lesser bond.
Set free my heart to seek the things beyond.
Deep on my forehead trace one shining name.
Burn, holy Flame! Burn on, thou living Flame!

Burn, holy Fire! Intensely glowing still,
Refine the steel! Possess and shape my will.
Be thou my goal, the whole of my desire.
Burn, holy Fire! Burn on, thou living Fire!

Burn, holy Light! Candescent in my soul,
Make me a lamp, transparent, clean, and whole.
Shed through my life thy splendor pure and white.
Burn, holy Light! Burn on, thou living Light! [1]

10. *Growing in Prayer*

> But when you pray, go into your room and
> shut the door and pray to your Father who
> is in secret; and your Father who sees in
> secret will reward you.
>
> MATT. 6:6 R.S.V.

Living in the presence of God, you begin to
realize that this *is* prayer, a way of life. Turning your
attention to God momentarily during the hours of a
busy day becomes a habit. You feel him near you and

[1] Grace S. Dawson, "Burn, Holy Light."

you look at things as you think he would see them.

Yet there is need for a special prayer time every day when you can be alone for a while, to bring your life to God. It is natural that you will grow in your prayer experience. Wise people have studied this experience of growth in prayer, and books have been written which can greatly help understanding. Sometimes prayer has been classified as two kinds: ordinary, which we may learn, and extraordinary, which God alone gives, and there are steps or degrees of each. The steps of ordinary prayer are four: (*a*) vocal prayer, (*b*) meditation, (*c*) affective prayer, and (*d*) the prayer of simple regard.

Vocal prayer, or verbal prayer, covers all with which we are most familiar in prayer. It begins with the prayers of the church ritual, such as the Lord's Prayer, recited aloud or prayed earnestly within our hearts. It continues with all the range of what John Magee calls "the spectrum of prayer." It moves through adoration, confession, petition, intercession, and thanksgiving. It includes all our attempts to put into words our relationship to the great God and Father of us all.

Reaching beyond verbal prayer is mental prayer, beginning with meditation. "Mental prayer," says John Magee, "is the classical name for the systematic use of imagination, will, feeling, and reason in meditation." [1] It is the focusing of the mind on some

[1] John Magee, *Reality and Prayer*, p. 179. Used by permission of Harper & Row, Publishers, Inc.

particular aspect of God or of the life of Christ or some kindred theme and the guiding of the thoughts around this theme. This takes long practice, for the thoughts are accustomed to wandering at random and will not be harnessed easily. This degree includes also meditated reading, or the slow repeating of the Lord's Prayer pondering on its meaning. There are different methods of meditation. Get one of the good books on prayer and study it.

One day, in the midst of your meditation, there may come over you a powerful lifting of the heart. You realize suddenly the holiness, the majesty of this wonderful Being before whom your heart is kneeling. You are filled with humility, with love, with a choking, almost hopeless longing. Words cease. You can no longer think, you can only feel. This is *affective prayer,* the prayer of the will, the prayer of the affections.

Then there may come a time when such a warm rush of feeling is followed by a quietness so deep that you feel no desire for words. You only look toward God with your whole soul, knowing that he knows all about you and that he is all you need. This is the *prayer of simple regard,* sometimes called the *prayer of simplicity.* It is the first experience of the prayer that is called contemplation. To remain thus quietly contemplating our Lord in all his greatness and beauty, asking for nothing, is a high experience, one which feeds the soul and helps it to grow.

Such is the ladder of prayer. It may be that you will have to go up and down the first two steps for many months or even years. On the other hand it may be that you will learn to pass after a brief period of meditation directly to the prayer of simple regard. Here, looking toward God, under whatever image you find him best, your activity will cease, and God's action will continue. For this is not idleness, although you are so quiet; it is God's opportunity to change you as he will and to give you what he has for you.

> This is sufficient prayer
> Only to speak his name
> And fix attention there,
> Lighted by that pure flame.
>
> Gracious before we plead,
> Let him correct the will
> And re-define the need;
> Say God, and then be still.[2]

Given the experience of the prayer of simple regard, we begin to understand a little of what is meant by the higher degrees of prayer experienced by the mystics. This path along which we have traveled a very little way stretches ahead, winding toward great heights of spiritual experience. Saints of all ages have traveled it and have left us their words of encouragement.

Our gracious Lord, the vision of these great spiritual heights makes us realize our own littleness and weakness. Give us small lessons to learn that we may not

[2] Elinor Lennen, "Adoration." Used by permission.

43

become discouraged. Grant us the light of thy daily presence as we strive to use what faith we have. AMEN.

11. *The High Path*

Whoso trusteth in the Lord, happy is he.
PROV. 16:20

Living in God's presence there comes into the soul's experience a real and deep contentment. The first adjustment has been made, the new outlook has become habitual, life holds a new solidity and peace. With God an actual sharer in the day's activities, there is a difference which can scarcely be described. We may do the same things as before, meet the same people, respond to the same demands on our time and energy. But there is a difference in the inner feeling-tone of the self which acts.

Fénelon said:

So let us scorn earthly things, to be wholly God's. I am not saying that we should leave them absolutely, because when we are already living an honest and regulated life, we need only to change our heart's depth in loving, and we shall do nearly the same things which we were doing. For God does not reverse the conditions of men, nor the responsibilities which he himself has given them, but we, to serve God, do what we were doing to serve and please the world, and to satisfy ourselves. There would be only this difference, that instead of being devoured by pride, . . . we shall act with

44

liberty, courage and hope in God. Confidence will animate us.[1]

Work is more satisfying, for it has become part of a larger plan. It is done with God's help and for his glory. We have learned to listen for guidance in time of doubt. We have found the secret of serenity in times of difficulty. Good things which come our way have an added richness, for we see in them now the gift of God. It is as if we have been climbing a slope and have come out on a high level, where the going is easier.

There is also the joy of sharing. When we overcome the old timidity and speak about our faith, we find that there is response from others. There are occasions when a word from us has been a help to someone else. This adds its own glow to our happiness.

Is it possible, then, that there could be a danger lurking in this happy situation? Have our adjustments been made too easily? Can it be that we might become careless in our attitude, that we might begin to take for granted the beloved companionship? Is there a possibility that a certain lethargy might overtake us, that we might become slack in our discipline, forgetful of keeping our periods of prayer?

Ah, there is very real peril here. We are only human, and it is easy to slip. We must remember that "the path winds upward all the way." It is not for us to

---

[1] François Fénelon, *Christian Perfection,* ed. Charles F. Whiston, p. 66. Used by permission of Harper & Row, Publishers, Inc.

linger on any plateau, no matter how pleasant. We must climb. We must be always ready to undertake the next task, no matter how reluctant we are for the effort or fearful for the results.

Perhaps God will remind us by some small shock that we are losing our alertness. Perhaps we need the prodding of a disappointment or two. "Watch and pray, that ye enter not into temptation." (Matt. 26:41.) Tranquillity can be a temptation to laziness. We still could lose the treasure we have gained.

There is another danger—the danger of complacency, self-satisfaction—the doorway through which the sly old devil of pride enters into the situation. Some small triumph, which would have been impossible in the old days, begins to seem our own achievement instead of the gracious inward work of our Lord. Indeed we need to be vigilant, to give the praise to him, to remember and rejoice in our need of him. Truly we must "watch and pray."

> Let me be never satisfied,
> Unloose my soul
> From flimsy garments of small pride
> Over a goal
> Already won.
>
> Let me not pause for dreams
> Over a task that seems
> Finished and done.
>
> Let me instead
> Climb cleanly in the sun
> Toward some still steeper height ahead.

Spur me with pain,
A kindly hurt
That will not suffer me remain
Inert.[2]

12. *The Sacred Commonplace*

Having gifts that differ according to the grace
given to us, let us use them: . . . if service, in our
serving; he who teaches, in his teaching; . . .
he who does acts of mercy, with cheerfulness.
ROM. 12:6-8 R.S.V.

Fénelon is right; the outward circumstances are
not very different after we begin to seek the deeper
life. "When we are already living an honest and
regulated life, we need only to change our heart's
depth in loving, and we shall do nearly the same
things which we were doing." For this reason it sometimes seems that we must be falling short of what
is expected of us. We feel that we ought to have
greater offerings to bring to our Lord. We ought to
be able to do something of greater consequence to
show our love.

The thing to remember is that it is God who has
put us where we are, and our gift to him is to do
what de Caussade calls "the duties of our state."

These duties are the most certain indications of the
will of God, and nothing should be preferred to them;
in fulfiling them there is nothing to be feared, no ex-
clusion or discrimination to be made; the moments de-

[2] Grace S. Dawson, "Aspiration."

47

voted to them are the most precious and salutary for the soul from the fact that she is sure of accomplishing the good pleasure of God.[1]

But these everyday duties can be transformed from within by doing them for God as our willing and glad service to him. Instead of taking them as dull matter of course, we can regard each one as an enterprise suggested and shared by God himself, something to be done here and now, especially appointed to us.

Faithfulness to daily work may be uninteresting, but it is no small offering. It is the gift God wants from us above all. The very fact that it is not always easy or pleasant makes it all the more precious. We need to enlist our imagination in order that we may think of ourselves as working in a larger environment than the house or the school, the study or the shop or the office, immediately around us.

There is a story of a man who walked among the workers in a medieval city engaged on a building project. He questioned one here and there as to what he was doing. This one answered that he was carrying material from this place to that. Another replied that he was cutting stone to a certain size. A third, looking up with a radiant smile, answered, "I am building a cathedral."

I pray these seeming-empty hands
Hold gifts as to the Lord,

[1] J. P. de Caussade, *Abandonment to Divine Providence*, p. 55. Used by permission of Benziger Brothers, Inc.

In service of a taut-pulled sheet,
A hospitable board.

I pray the routine chore I do,
The dull task and the hard,
May seem to him who knows the wish
My broken cruse of nard.[2]

The housewife can then realize that she is preparing food and comfort for the Lord, who said "Inasmuch." The teacher can look upon her pupils, unruly ones and all, as belonging to God and entrusted to her care. The doctor can appreciate his high calling as healer of bodies and minds, often of souls as well. Executive, clerk, lawyer, mechanic, secretary, we are all engaged in carrying on God's business, and our loyalty is to him. It is he who takes note of the quality of our work and seals it with his approval.

This is, in a way, sacramental living. A sacrament is a symbolic act having a sacred significance. Living in daily companionship with God, everything we do can be lifted into his presence, and will take on new meaning. A routine meal becomes a true sacrament by a special grace, "Father, as this food nourishes our bodies, do thou feed our souls with thy Holy Spirit." This is and should be the purpose of the simplest grace before meals.

Life with all its variety, its grim and gracious aspects, its chores, and its challenges is a gift from

[2] Dorothy Brown Thompson, "Grace in Homespun." Used by permission.

God. Only as we accept it at its highest value and use it worthily are we expressing our gratitude for it.

Father, accept our lives and our service, such as they are. Take our daily work as done to thy glory. These daily gifts are all we have to give; bless them and bless us in the giving with thy joy and thy peace. AMEN.

13. *Answered Prayer*

And, I say unto you, Ask, and it shall be given you; seek, and ye shall find.   LUKE 11:9

The life lived with God is a life of answered prayer. It may take us months or years to realize the truth of this statement. For it is only through a deepening understanding of prayer that we begin to know this. It seems many times that the prayer we pray has no answer that we can understand.

A little boy prayed fervently for a pony. After some days his mother, fearing his disillusionment, asked him whether God had answered his prayer. "Oh, yes," said the child. "He said, 'No.'" There is truth here, for often in our asking we face the fact that the answer is apparently "No," or "Not yet."

This was what happened to Paul when he prayed about his "thorn in the flesh." No one knows whether this was a physical disability or a spiritual trial, but it troubled him sorely. "Three times I besought the Lord about this . . . ; but he said to me, 'My grace is sufficient for you, for my power is made perfect in weakness.'" (II Cor. 12:8-9 R.S.V.) Doubtless we too need to learn the lesson of humility and dependence upon God. We are not yet ready for another answer.

Sometimes we pray for definite things instead of for the real need which lies behind. A woman who needed to go many places for her work prayed for a car of her own. It seemed the only way to satisfy the situation. But as she thought it over she realized that what she needed was simply transportation, so she formed a different prayer. Years passed and still she had no car, but she had found every need for transportation met, by friends or other arrangements. The real desire was fulfilled.

Lynn J. Radcliffe says:

All prayer is answered. The answer is the experience of God himself, sometimes manifested through the release of new energies within us, sometimes revealed through the action of God's other children who come to our aid, sometimes released in the change of the situation itself through God's creative action upon it, sometimes unveiled in the ultimate answer which He is unfolding, and sometimes discovered in a new consciousness of His powerful Presence by our side.[1]

It all comes back to the discovery of prayer as a *way of life*. If we live day by day in communion with God, our needs are made known almost involuntarily

[1] *Making Prayer Real* (Apex ed.; Nashville: Abingdon Press, 1961), p. 70.

and are met by his constant watchful care. We encounter difficulties but their menace becomes less in the presence of his love. If confused, we know that the confusion will gradually clear in the divine light, and, listening, we become aware of the course to pursue. This is not uncertain hypothesis. It is the witness of multitudes who have walked this way before us.

> I prayed that God would take away
> The griefs that seemed too great to bear;
> He left my sorrows, but he gave
> Me strength to carry all their care.
>
> I asked for light; he let me grope
> In darkness, till with inner sight,
> I learned that even darkness may,
> To one who trusts in God, be light.[2]

No, it cannot be said that the way we walk, even with God, is a way free from suffering. There are periods of darkness, elements of tragedy to be encountered, soul-shaking disasters to be lived through. For this is truly life. Christ himself met disappointment, loneliness, and the dark disaster of betrayal. He never promised his followers freedom from trouble, quite the contrary.

Moreover it is through meeting pain and difficulty that the spirit grows. Too often we forget this. We pray for our children to become strong men and

[2] Clara Aiken Speer, "Answered Prayer." Used by permission.

women, mature and wise. Yet we shrink from the blows that fall on them and cry out for their comfort and peace. We should pray, rather, for their awareness of the inner Reality which will enable them to accept the suffering without bitterness and through it to attain greater strength and nobler height.

For the glorious thing about it is the presence of God himself in the midst of the suffering, sharing the sorrow, striving with the difficulty, lifting the burden. This is what becomes clearer the longer we walk in this beloved companionship. There is light in the darkness and peace in the midst of peril. Life has a new dimension, unknown to those who walk another way.

Teach us, O God, the true meaning of the life of prayer. Lead us to that higher place where we find in thee the answer to all our needs and the key to the abundant and victorious life. AMEN.

14. *The Thankful Heart*

In every thing give thanks: for this is the will of God in Christ Jesus concerning you.
I THESS. 5:18

God wants joy and thanksgiving from us. To this end he has given us life itself—life in the world—and the senses to receive and enjoy it. Think what that means! Think of the world itself, all around us, for seeing and hearing, smelling and touching!

53

Lift your eyes to the rich blue of the sky and be-hold the rolling, shifting, changing clouds, bearing over the earth their bounty of moisture for all living things. Consider a tree, an oak or maple, wide spread-ing with leafy shadows; or a majestic cedar, its boughs holding a winter burden of snow; or a slender palm, fronds swaying in tropic breezes. These are sights of sheer beauty to the eyes and meaning to the mind.

Think of rolling plains, green and gold with ripen-ing grain; of fruit trees with their beautiful largess reddening to the harvest. Think of forests; of birds winging their way across the land, bringing spring songs and the twittering of feathered hosts. Think of rivers watering the earth and winding to the sea. Think of flowering gardens perfuming the night air, the grace of blossoming deserts after winter rains, the small flowers unfolding along the wayside. All this beauty we have been given and eyes and ears to receive freely its loveliness wherever we go. Thank God for the beauty of this world!

God made the world and gave it to us for creative use; this is also a world of men and women. Note the different types of people. Think of the old men whose life-span is nearly over; of little bright-haired children, shouting with fun and running just because they can; of women with kind faces; of young people, absorbed in themselves and their plans. This is a world of people, and it is our privilege to know them, work with them, enjoy them, help those whose need is before us. Thank God for human relationships!

Consider life itself! Remember how you felt growing up, how slowly the year seemed to go to the next birthday when you would be a year older. Remember the eagerness on meeting each new school environment, and the thrill of graduating and entering the world of the adult. Recall your first experience of earning your own money. Consider the many friendships that have come your way, each one different. Think of the varied relationships you have had, with family and with friends. These are treasures; they have had a part in your life, have helped to shape you. Thank God for all of them!

Be grateful for difficult experiences, as well as pleasant ones. Were you ever hurt, baffled, and frustrated by seemingly unjust treatment? Could you rise above it? Did you learn any lesson from the circumstances? Remember the fellow worker with an oversensitive or thorny disposition. Did you suffer from his hurt feelings, his vindictiveness? Were you able to understand the *why* of the sensitiveness, so that you could ward off the blow? These things all make for growth. Even such experiences are part of a full, well-rounded life. We can learn to accept them as the seasoning of our life.

Thinking seriously about life's unfolding experiences; it is possible to consider them honestly as all good, or good for us. Isn't it true that fullness of life is what we want—a little of everything, the bitter with the sweet, the danger surmounted, the problem solved? There is the crux, the solving of problems. Mankind has always advanced through the solving of his problems. We see it in the individuals around us. A weak character rallies to meet a problem and achieves a degree of strength. A strong character grows stronger through solving his problems and often turns to seek out greater problems.

> Here then are gifts in bountiful tide,
> Plentiful, lavish, deep, high, and wide.
> How shall we use them that still they may bless?
> Season them well with thankfulness.[1]

Best of all, never forget what a part love plays in your life. What is love? Love is *goodwill* of many degrees and variations. We have had the warm, tender affection of parents, of husband or wife, of the dear close friend. We have had the salty, bracing goodwill of brothers and sisters, cousins, schoolmates, co-workers. We have known the warm, responsive appeal of little children, of pupils perhaps. We have had the grateful appreciation from those it has been our joy to help. Be soundly grateful for the love in our lives.

We thank thee, Lord, for life in this world of thine, for all its colors and kinds of experience, for all its good and gracious gifts. For fullness of life, we thank thee, Lord. AMEN.

---

[1] Clara Aiken Speer, "The Saving Salt." Used by permission.

15. *The Holy Spirit*

If you then, who are evil, know how to give good gifts to your children, how much more will the heavenly Father give the Holy Spirit to those who ask him?   LUKE 11:13 R.S.V.

When God created he put himself into his creation. From within creation the creative spirit of God went on building, from the lowest levels of the inorganic world into the realm of living things, from the simplest forms of plant and animal life to the higher forms where intelligence begins to show through, to man himself in the image of God capable of thinking and loving. We call this evolution, but it is truly the Spirit of God, creating from within, working toward the two goals of truth and love.

Every creature God made has two urges: to become a complete individual, and to relate itself to other individuals around it to make a larger whole. This is the double goal of the Spirit working within, to be whole and to belong, completeness and love. We have these same longings too. Each of us wants to be a full person, to fulfill the law within, to be the biggest person possible. And each of us wants to belong, to have warm relationships with others, to experience love. These urges indicate the Spirit working within us. But we have a choice. We can blunder along toward our goals alone, or we can accept the guidance and help within.

The creating Spirit worked through the ages to make man capable of reflecting God's nature. At last the time came when God could create for himself a new channel of love and truth. God walked the earth in the person of Christ, sharing all the limitations and burdens we have to bear. Supreme truth crowned his words so that men marveled at him. Supreme love shone in his look and his actions to those who drew near.

And it is through Christ that the invitation comes, the invitation to the divine companionship. "I will pray the Father," he said, "and he will give you another Counselor, to be with you for ever, even the Spirit of truth." "If I do not go away, the Counselor will not come to you; but if I go, I will send him to you." (John 14:16; 16:7 R.S.V.)

This then is the blessed truth; the Counselor whom God will send is the very Spirit who dwelt in Christ. The Holy Spirit of the creative God has walked the earth as man, taking into himself all human experience, even unto betrayal and death. In Christ he has overcome evil and suffering. In Christ he has lived his way through to us. This is the Counselor God gives us as a friend and companion. If we ask him and allow him he will possess our lives and make them strong and beautiful with truth and love.

We do not know just how he does this, and we cannot measure our progress at all. We can only rejoice in his presence, listen to his guidance, and keep ourselves aware and obedient. He must do the rest. He will make us what he wishes us to be. He will use us in spite of our imperfections.

There are still plenty of imperfections. The old nature underneath crops out very often. We falter and stumble and fail in our good intentions, for the

58

old self is still self-centered and willful. But the Counselor within will help us to conquer the tendency of the lower self to betray us. We can only ask forgiveness for the mistakes and wrongdoing and go steadily onward. We can only trust the Father that through his grace the Spirit will be able to make us more Christlike and use us even as we are for his purposes. If God had to wait for perfect instruments to accomplish his purposes, his work would never be done. He does his creative work subject to the limitations of his creation, and in us subject to our human limitations.

> God, make my life a book
> Wherein you write
> For men to read wherever I may go
> The poem of your presence.
>
> God, make my life a window,
> Crystal clear
> As truth made simple for the mind of childhood,
> That eyes may see through me
> The strength and understanding of your heart.
>
> God, make my life a garden,
> Planted and tended daily by your hand,
> Wherein souls walking
> May find care comforted,
> Faith flowering in the sunny light of hope,
> And in the center
> An ever-springing fountain of your love.[1]

[1] Grace S. Dawson, "Consecration."

16. *Humility and Peace*

Thou wilt keep him in perfect peace, whose mind is
stayed on thee: because he trusteth in thee.

Isa. 26:3

Why is it that our peace of heart is so often shattered, even when we are trying to live in communion
with the Spirit of God? Is it not often because of our
impatience? It seems to us that we progress very
slowly, that we are at a standstill in the inner life.
The things we have tried to accomplish, the ideals we
have striven to achieve, remain unrealized. We look
around and see much to be done; we feel the urge to
help, to be used for others, and yet we seem to come
no nearer our desire. We are as sluggish and faulty
as ever.

Is it possible that this impatience really stems from
a kind of pride? We had expected to accomplish
things more quickly. We are impatient at our own
slowness, which we find hard to understand. We are
troubled that our spiritual life does not prove more
fruitful. Then we are troubled at the notion of being
troubled. Where is the "peace that passeth understanding"?

When this mood overtakes us it is time to look
to God and ask him to teach us new lessons of
patience and humility. This he is doing all the time
through the great pageant of the universe around
us, if we will but consider it.

"The heavens declare the glory of God; and the
firmament showeth his handiwork. Day unto day
uttereth speech, and night unto night showeth knowl-

edge." (Ps. 19:1-2.) Steadily the earth revolves. Every morning the sunlight returns again, and every night the continents are wrapped in the shadows of sleep.

Growth is everywhere—in the mighty trees and just as surely in the small flowers along the garden path. But life knows its own rhythms, rest and growth, the fallow period and the fruitful cycle. All is in order and has its own pattern. Each of us has a pattern too in which impatience has no place.

Who feels conceit when he measures his span
With the height of the heavenly arch?
Or anger, making him less than a man
When he watches the calm stars march?

Who dares to balk at order and law
When he sees how the suns obey?
Whose heart is so pure as to feel no flaw
When he looks at the Milky Way?

Whose pride of power withstands a show
Of lightning, dazzling and strange?
Whose jewels compare with the diamonded snow?
Whose voice with the wind's range?

"When I consider the firmament,"
World crowded, rim after rim,
"What is man," O Lord of the sky,
"That thou are mindful of him?" [1]

We live in a world today that is filled with frustra-

[1] May Williams Ward, "Consider the Sky." Used by permission.

61

tion and knows little stability. Each of us must find for himself the inner peace he needs. Consider this world created by God, a world of order and beauty. Consider the "calm stars," the eternal seas, the winds that follow their pattern around the earth, the processional of the seasons with seedtime and harvest. These are God's parables for our teaching.

Be content to be small, one of the multitude, yet not neglected nor overlooked by the great creative God. Be content to see your life as a fragment of a vast plan which is working itself out in order under the guidance of God. Be content to feel yourself dependent on a great wisdom which waits to help you with your own small problems. Realize that God has not forgotten his children, that the world is in his keeping, that the laws of the human heart are likewise true and abiding, and that in the end justice will prevail.

Try to step aside now and then from the rush and hurry of life, and learn to listen and wait. Contemplate the growth of a tree, year by year putting forth its leaves to sunshine and rain, and enlarging the circle of its trunk by a mere line. Realize the patience of God, the humility of God, accomplishing his work within the circumference of his own laws. These are the things which make for humility, and in humility there is peace.

O God, how great is thy patience with us! Teach us to listen to thee and allow our lives to be filled and guided. Stay our minds on thee and keep us in thy peace. AMEN.

WHEN
SHADOWS
COME

17. *The Desert Trail*

The wilderness and the solitary place shall be
glad for them; and the desert shall rejoice, and
blossom as the rose.　　　　　　　　Isa. 35:1

When you have been walking in the way of
prayer for months, or even years, something distressing
may happen. The way may lead through a desert
area, where all the thrill of life has vanished. Your
days are not only monotonous, they are gray and
bleak and dry. All that you do appears to be useless,
an empty business of going through motions, and
you wonder where all the peace and joy of the divine
companionship has gone.

The feeling of being near God grows dim, and you
find little comfort in prayer. It is impossible to medi-
tate anymore, and vocal prayers are halting, until you
wonder if you are just saying words without meaning. Service to others which you enjoyed becomes
tasteless, and the glow of life seems to have left you.

Wise teachers tell us not to be surprised at such

"dry" times. All the saints have had them, sometimes
for long periods. No one knows just why they come
or why they sometimes last so long. Look conscien-
tiously for some reason in your outer life.

First of all, are you physically in good health? Sick
people have sick thoughts, and some bodily lack may
be at the root of emotional depression. Lift your
physical need to the healing God, and listen to his
guidance. Perhaps you need more rest, or perhaps, on
the contrary, you need more exercise. Perhaps you
need the attention of a physician.

Then it is well to survey your relationships to
others. Is there something here that needs repairing—
a little discontentment, a small resentment, a disappointment, something rankling just below the surface which has clouded over the whole sky? Pray to
be shown the reason if there is one, and ask God what
to do about it. Tell him quite honestly just how you
feel, and ask his help in setting yourself right.

If the dryness persists, and there seems neither reason nor remedy, try not to rebel nor to despair. The
only thing to do is just to accept it as something God
wants you to have, something which will have its
own lesson to teach. You need not know the reason,
only that his love will take care of you. You will be
given strength to go on and understanding, if it is
God's will for you. Continue faithful in the "duties of
your state," and hold to your prayer habits as well as
may be without worrying about how good your prayer
is. Whether the dryness lasts a few days or for months,

whether it is quiet and dull or stormy with trials, there will come an end in God's own time.

It may help to think of it as a time of winter in your life, when the creative forces are in abeyance for a period of rest. God has not deserted you. He has written for us a parable of the seasons, where winter is followed by spring with its Easter renewal of glowing life. He will give you an Easter at last. Consider the suspended life of the wintry world.

Humble with emptiness and gray with dearth,
Swept clean by twisting tempest, now the earth,
Kneeling for absolution, knows within
New pulses where the chill of death has been;
Awaits a benediction, then, grown bold,
Dons the rose-bordered robe, the ring of gold
The Father gives
The prodigal who lives.

Then let me wait, feeling within the stir
Of new things growing where the withered were,
Feeling the tides of Easter flow across
My heavy consciousness of lack and loss.
Then let me stand, tall in the rain-washed air,
With lifted head again, eager to wear
Like spring
The new robe and the ring.[1]

We have learned that all experience contributes to growth, often we grow most by the difficult things.

[1] Grace S. Dawson, "At Easter." Used by permission of *Unity*, published by Unity School of Christianity, Kansas City, Missouri.

Accept the dark wintry period, and what joy to come back into the radiance of the God-filled life! Severe winters are followed by the keenest rush of new life in spring. So it will be with God's springtime in your heart.

Our Father, if we must go through a winter of the soul, bless the growth of new life underneath. Enable us to gain from our own suffering a deep sympathy with the trials of others. And give us by thy grace a new springtime of life. AMEN.

18. *The Stumbling*

I do not understand my own actions. For I do not do what I want, but I do the very thing I hate.
ROM. 7:15 R.S.V.

Walking in the light is its own reward. The companionship of God makes life a more satisfying thing. Hard tasks are easier, and difficult situations have a way of opening out into solutions. But sometimes I become lulled into a false security, and I get a rude shock. Suddenly I catch myself doing something which I know is wrong. I am faced with a situation in which I have to choose between doing a friendly thing for a stranger and carrying out undisturbed my plans which include a few intimate friends. I must make up my mind on the instant, and I choose my own plans.

Too late I realize this, and I cannot forget it. I

have done something mean. I have betrayed my Master, who said, "As you did it to one of the least of these my brethren, you did it to me" (Matt. 25:40 R.S.V.). I have refused to include Christ among my friends! Remorse overwhelms me and my own plans rebuke me. I see how I could have adjusted the plans to include the stranger. The whole episode was an opportunity for enrichment. And I refused it.

"Let any one who thinks that he stands take heed lest he fall." (I Cor. 10:12 R.S.V.) I have done something for which I am terribly sorry. The worst of it is I knew better. I was taken off guard. My self-confidence is shaken. How can I think myself a true Christian when I can so easily forget my ideals?

I prayed for courage, but it was denied;
I shrank from danger when it found my side.

I prayed for sympathy, but could not speak
Compassion to the unattractive weak.

I prayed for tenderness, but fled the knife
That would have made me sensitive to life.

I prayed, and then refused the things I sought;
I did not know they were so dearly bought.[1]

That is the crux of the matter—I did not know. I had always thought I would do the right thing. I did not realize that temptation would take me un-

[1] Elinor Lennen, "Ye Know Not What Ye Ask." Used by permission.

aware. The unfortunate incident sticks in the mind like a thorn and will not be forgotten.

I wonder how it must look to God. How can he take my prayers seriously when my actions say I am not sincere? But I *was* sincere. I *do* want to live the life of love and truth. I want to face whatever comes with kindness and courage. How can I account for my failure?

It is an old question. Paul faced it again and again. "I do not do what I want, but I do the very thing I hate." It is the same old self within me coming unexpectedly through. I did not know it would happen, but God knew it, even when I started on this inward and upward path.

God does not show us all our weakness at the beginning. If he did we would likely be too discouraged to start at all. He reveals our faults to us a little at a time, as we can stand it. This has been a revealing incident. It shows up a real weakness, which has no doubt caused me to stumble often when I have not seen it so clearly. What shall I do about it now that I have fallen flat? There are several things to do in order to regain my footing.

First, I must acknowledge the wrong, face it exactly as it is. An opportunity has been irretrievably lost, for I cannot even apologize. The same chance will not come again. My thoughts turn to Peter, denying his Lord. No wonder he went out and wept bitterly. Poor, impulsive Peter!

Second, I must repent, which I truly do, and confess and ask forgiveness of God. I must not do this too lightly, knowing that God will forgive; but I must do it in a spirit of contrition, resolving not to let this same temptation get the better of me again. I must remember to ask forgiveness for the pride which made me depend on myself.

Third, I must *accept* God's forgiveness and forgive myself. My memory of the mistake will remain to prick me with remorse. But this must not hamper or embitter or discourage me. I must accept forgiveness freely and stand up and go on, less sure of my own strength, more sensitive to the divine touch. Thus I will find again the joy of being understood by the divine love.

Lord, be very near us in the time of our falling. Replace our broken self-confidence by confidence in thee. Forgive us once again, and teach us by our own need of forgiveness how to forgive others. AMEN.

19. *Meeting Loneliness*

I will not leave you desolate; I will come to you.
JOHN 14:18 R.S.V.

Man was not made to be alone. In early times man lived a clan life, a tribal life, in which individuality was merged in the group. Activities were group activities, and the purposes and triumphs belonged to the group as a whole. It is only as groups became nations and civilization advanced that the contrary movement made itself felt. And only in recent times has individuality become important.

Today in democratic and Christian countries individuality is stressed. Christ taught the infinite value of each human life, and this is part of our heritage. But human nature retains the old need for sharing. We need one another. The human heart seeks fellowship.

We like to share our activities, to do things together with a common purpose. There is enjoyment in the interchange of thoughts and ideas and the working toward completion of a task. We want to share our happiness with someone who will rejoice with us. And we especially need to share our sorrows and find comfort in the consolation of those who care. We still need to "belong."

But life moves on and is not always kind. Changes come, new circumstances in our restless civilization move us about, and we find ourselves losing friends who have filled a big place in our lives. Or death knocks at the door, and a dear one is gone. We miss the hand that touched ours, the eyes that looked into ours with love and laughter and understanding. Gone is the meaning of life and its purposive zest.

Loneliness is a burden that can be very heavy, and some lives seem to have more than their share of this burden to carry. Getting up in the morning alone, going through a lonely program, with many meals alone—this can become a drab and sorry business.

Thirty or forty years ago a little book in the popular vogue told the story of a young girl who was overcome with shyness and loneliness. A friend gave her a secret formula which transformed her life and gave her the courage to offer friendliness, with its sure return in happiness, wherever she went. The secret was, "Everybody's lonesome."

There is a great truth in that simple statement. There is a very real sense in which every soul goes a lonely way. We cannot tell from external appearances how near the surface that loneliness may be. He who reaches out a kindly hand to another may unknowingly be healing a real hurt in that other's life. "The way to have friends is yourself to be a friend." A popular song has it: "Love is not love until you give it away."

Then there is above all the supreme Companionship. If this means much to the normal life, how incomparably much more must it mean to a truly lonely life! And yet it is possible for people to struggle through a dark and desolate period without realizing that God is truly near, waiting to comfort and bless.

Where once my sluggard eyes have slept
Like Jacob, now I kneel to pray,
And "Surely God is in this place,"
In wonder I have learned to say.

How often have I closed my eyes
To him who was forever near.
How often have my ears been dull
Because I did not want to hear.

Oh, stupid to deny myself
The Father's comfort and his grace,

Then murmur that "I knew it not,"
While he abides in every place.[1]

He does abide in every place. He is there to answer when I call. If I do not find him it is because I do not seek patiently. "Seek and you shall find," said the Lord. Thousands have found it true. There is a depth and sweetness to the divine friendship which is indescribable to those who know it not.

"Mother, don't go away," said a little girl going to bed. "I shall be lonesome."

"God is with you, dear," said Mother.

"Yes, I know," said the child. "But I want somebody with a face."

This is a human need, too. But the beautiful truth is that God knows this, and most often he makes himself known to us through human love and nearness. Prayer is surely one answer to loneliness.

Our Father, help us to heal our own loneliness by ministering to the need of others, and thus prove ourselves worthy to be called thy children. AMEN.

20. *The Shadow of Doubt*

I have chosen the way of truth.
Ps. 119:30

It is almost inconceivable that after years of living in the companionship of the Spirit of God there

[1] Elinor Lennen, "God of the Lonely Places." Used by permission.

should come times of doubt. Yet this can happen, and it can happen to you. It may be that you have heard some convincing speaker utter words that set your mind in turmoil. Or the newspaper with its daily record of strife, disaster, revolt, and cruelty has darkened your outlook until there seems no hope. Or some book written lucidly and emphatically indicates that man himself is the only hope; he has worked his way up to reason, and he must find his own way out of the world's difficulties to whatever goal lies ahead—if there is a goal.

These are plausible considerations, and it is hard not to be swayed by them. You find your faith in an ever-ruling Providence tottering. The world seems an alien place, and you wonder if religion is just a fantasy, and you and your trusting friends are dupes of the imagination. A cloud of doubt hangs over you, and life seems suddenly a futile thing.

What can you do? Pray. If prayer seems absurd without faith, pray anyway. "Lord, I believe, help thou my unbelief." Pray for patience to wait until the cloud passes over. For it will pass if you hold on. Pray for help and guidance. It will come—from some wise friend, or some illuminating statement in book or periodical. Others are in doubt too. Many conflicting beliefs and declarations are afloat around us. Pray to be made strong again in your own faith. Perhaps help will come from the Rosary of Song, as it did to me, in the words of a beautiful old poem sung to the music of "Finlandia."

73

Be still, my soul: thy God doth undertake
To guide the future as He has the past.
Thy hope, thy confidence let nothing shake;
All now mysterious shall be bright at last.
Be still, my soul: the waves and winds still know
His voice who ruled them while He dwelt below.[1]

Remember that you have chosen your way, "the
way of truth," by accepting Christ as your Master.
"I am the way, the truth, and the life," he said.
Christ's whole life was built and lived on faith. Faith
is a key word of the New Testament. Over and
over it falls from his lips, "According to your faith
be it unto you."

Christ is the supreme Teacher. Men who listened
to his words marveled at his wisdom, down to earth
practical, yet high as heaven ineffable. That wisdom
has never been surpassed. And that wisdom em-
phasized the power of faith. Did you turn aside from
his counsel to give credence to some prophet who
cannot see beyond this generation? Listen then to a
great scientist of our generation in refutation.

The order of the world is no accident. . . . The kingdom of heaven is not the isolation of good from evil. It
is the overcoming of evil by good. This transmutation
of evil into good enters into the actual world by reason
of the inclusion of the nature of God, which includes
the ideal vision of each actual evil so met with a novel
consequent as to issue in the restoration of goodness.[2]

[1] Katharine Von Schlegel, 1697.
[2] Alfred North Whitehead, *Religion in the Making.* Used by
permission of Harper & Row, Publishers, Inc.

God can meet even evil creatively and turn it to good.

Said Mahatma Gandhi, "He who would in his own person test the fact of God's presence, can do so by a living faith. Exercise of faith will be safest where there is a clear determination summarily to reject all that is contrary to Truth and Love." [3]

> Not metal compass, stars, nor sun
> Can guide the spirit daring the unknown,
> So that the journey may be safely run;
> This venture hangs upon one Power alone.
> When labyrinth of inmost tangled thought
> Gives wilderness outside its counterpart,
> Then must the certain and the true be sought,
> And one Voice only counsel the deep heart.
> By day, by night, we go not anywhere
> But in his world surrounded by his care. [4]

So it all comes back to faith, a faith in God, and in Christ who assures us that God is a God of love. This is our foundation stone. On this alone we can build.

O God, who in Christ sounded the depth and heights of human experience, thou knowest our weakness. Strengthen our faith. Be with us when the cloud of doubt overshadows us, show us thy light still shining, and lead us through the darkness. AMEN.

[3] From *Mahatma Gandhi* by C. F. Andrews. Used by permission of The Estate of C. F. Andrews.

[4] Elinor Lennen, "Assurance." Used by permission.

21. *The Shadow of Death*

Though I walk through the valley of the shadow
of death, I will fear no evil.   Ps. 23:4

Death is always a shadow—a sobering, saddening thing. When a life has been ended in early youth or in its prime, there is sorrow for the unfulfilled promise. We think of the learning years, the potential ready to be realized, apparently wasted by the sharp cutting off of the life-span. What we cannot know is the possible use of that potential in another realm of the spirit, now veiled from us.

When a leader of great influence is taken away before his work is accomplished, the loss to this world is hard to estimate. This was the situation when all nations sorrowed at the death of Dag Hammarskjold, whose integrity and earnestness stood so valiantly against chaos in the Congo. What could compensate for such a loss?

But death comes closest to us in the passing of a dearly loved presence from our lives, leaving a vacant place of loneliness which nothing can fill. Where there is no hope of a future life the shadow is black indeed. In the Christian communion, however, there is this hope to hold, that spirit is more vital than flesh and does not perish, that the loved one has gone on to a new environment and a richer experience.

Such a hope makes it illogical to grieve for the one who is gone. But grief is not logical, it is too intensely emotional to reason itself away. We know we are grieving for our own loneliness, but the pang is too keen to be allayed. The pattern of our own life is broken and cannot be mended. Words of comfort and assurance are clutched at eagerly, but they cannot fill the void. The wound gapes and no power on earth can heal its soreness. The heart must make its own adjustment, and sometimes that comes slowly.

Then it is that the Christian cherishes the faith that life goes on, that the spirit of the dear one is alive, sentient, somehow still present to those left behind. There is a definite confidence that is the possession of many bereaved persons.

A widow was visited by a woman with a small child.

"Where is Mr. S?" asked the little boy.

"He is not here now," replied the widow quietly.

"But where is he?" persisted the child.

The mother made no attempt to intervene, so the widow answered from her heart. "He has gone to heaven to live with God, but he is still near me."

A faith of this kind is a living testimony to the power of Christian thought through the centuries. Surely this must be the meaning of the old phrase "the communion of saints." Those no longer living in the body are nevertheless here in this world, alive in the spirit, surrounding us with their love, their watchful care, their happy "communion."

> "I heard that you had lost him" so I said,
>   Thinking, somehow, it was a softer phrase
>   And trying to avoid by devious ways
> The starkness of the blunt word "He is dead."

"Would you," she answered, "say, if he had crossed
The ocean, I had lost him? This is just
A wider ocean, spanned by love and trust.
He is dead—yes. Thank God, he is not lost." [1]

In the deeper life, lived in companionship with
God, we know we can turn to the strong, warm love
of a Father and pour out our sorrow and be understood. Only those who have passed through such an
experience can know the comfort of being understood. And by the same token, we realize slowly
that we have a gift—understanding—to give to another whose heart is sore. This is something, to be
able to say to a grief-bowed friend, "I know what you
are going through. I understand. I can tell you that,
though the scar remains, time will ease the soreness."

As for the future, we need not be able to make a
concrete picture of what it holds. Enough for us that
the earthly parting is not the end of the story.
Enough for us that "Christ has been raised from the
dead, the first fruits of those who have fallen asleep"
(I Cor. 15:20 R.S.V.).

*Our Father, we thank thee that beyond the shadow
shines the light eternal, and that in that light we may
feel the living presence of the spirit of our loved ones.
Bless every yearning heart with the comforting sense
of thy nearness and the knowledge of thy care.* AMEN.

---

[1] Dorothy Brown Thompson, "For Eternity." Used by permission.

22. *The Shadow of Judas*

In my distress I cried unto the Lord,
and he heard me.   Ps. 120:1

What distress is like that of a friend's betrayal?
How can we receive a blow from one we have loved
and trusted and not feel that all life has failed us?
Friendship is one of the richest and most treasured
of possessions; how can we go on unscathed when
friendship proves false?

This is one of the hard problems of life, one which
almost everyone must meet in some form. Fortunate
is the person to whom it comes not too severely, an
offense which is not too grave. Perhaps the offender
realizes his fault and asks forgiveness. With God's
help this situation can be met and mended. The
fault is pardoned and the friendship is restored. Sometimes there is even a greater depth to the relationship
after the wound is healed. It is as if a testing time
has proved something worthy of another chance.
Jesus forgave Peter and received a lifetime of loyal
service.

But too often betrayal ends the trust and shocks the
love beyond repair. Too often penitence does not
follow, forgiveness is not asked, and something has
been killed that once was living and strong. What
can we do about such a disaster, so that it does not
spoil our life and our faith in all mankind?

How can one love and trust again when human
nature has proved too weak to be worthy of trust?
The temptation is to withdraw into oneself and re-
fuse to give that trust again to anyone. This is to

punish oneself indeed. This is to deny oneself for always the blessing of friendship, the joy of mutual benefits and outgoing experience.

This hurt goes far too deep to ever heal;
Time has no balm to take away its throb.
Aching remembrance will forever rob
The bruised heart of the trust the unscarred feel.
A horse would sicken Trojans, once betrayed.
Had Caesar lived and friendship died instead
Who knows how many faithful would have bled
Because of Brutus? Thus the price is paid.

For he who once has known the bargained kiss
That marks betrayal is not free again
From sick imaginings; is wary when
New friendship buds. The black result is this:
Because he smarts from one false, nettled grasp
There will be hands that he will fear to clasp.[1]

There lies another sad result of such an attitude, injustice to others, the turning away from what would be a true and faithful relationship. This must not be. Two things we must try to do: first, forgive the offender even if he does not ask it. This is hard, and we need God's help. We need to look behind the act to the motive or the situation which led to the act. We need to put this in the hands of the loving Father who has often had to forgive us, remembering that

[1] Velma West Sykes, "Long Shadow of Judas." Used by permission.

80

we pray, "Forgive us as we forgive." Thus we cleanse the heart of bitterness and antagonism.

Then it may begin to seem possible to look once more for trustworthy and firm friendship. It is there to be found. All humankind is not unworthy just because one person has played us false. Life has other treasure for us, if we do not close our eyes and our hearts.

> One friend may disappoint or grieve,
> Since mortal flesh and will are frail,
> But friendship's total can retrieve
> Loss when a comrade seems to fail.
>
> Count lifetime revenue before
> You charge dismay against a friend;
> Hearts mine a richer vein of ore
> Than any two can comprehend.[2]

For the most worthwhile things in life some risk must be run. We must give ourselves to receive the best. And if we have done this in vain in one instance, we must not let it prevent us from finding recompense in a richer and deeper experience. Love is still the most valuable thing in the world. We must not let one loss ruin our chances of mining "a richer vein of ore."

God, with such a hurt where can we go but to thee, the unfailing friend? Give us the grace to forgive,

[2] Elinor Lennen, "Richer Vein." Used by permission.

*and the strength and courage to forget the hurt and
reach out once more for the gift of human friendship.*
AMEN.

23. *Facing Fear*

Fear not, for I am with you,
be not dismayed, for I am your God.
Ps. 41:10 R.S.V.

No life is a stranger to fear. Nor is fear always a
bad thing. There is fear of external things which
affects our outer life. Such fear makes us take proper
precautions for safety for ourselves and others. For
fear of accidents we obey traffic laws, keep our car
in good condition, and take out insurance. Fear of
disease impels us to proper diet, sensible living habits,
periodic check-ups with the doctor. Right fears help
us to organize our lives so that fear is minimized.

Other fears we learn to conquer and live with.
Learning to swim reduces fear of the water. Some
people fear high places and avoid them. Others fear
being shut in and learn to disregard such an attitude.
There are scores of small fears which have a place in
human life, and to which we adjust.

But there are other fears which dwell in the inner
life, subtler, based on inner problems. There is the
fear of failure, which limits our undertakings and
hampers our best attempts to do something worthwhile. There is a fear of what people will say, con-

trolling our actions. This may be a cowardly fear. We do not speak out for our ideals because we fear adverse criticism or ridicule. This fear we should acknowledge, and overcome it with the help of the Spirit of truth.

Fear of closeness to other people, says a psychologist, is one of the commonest fears. Such a fear usually arises from a hurt received from friend or relative. The victim is put on the defensive and shrinks from any other intimacy for fear of being hurt again. Perhaps this has happened to you. What can you do?

The way to eliminate any fear is first to face it frankly. Sometimes the fear is hidden and you need help in hunting it down and bringing it out into the light. When it is discovered and laid bare the way to healing is open. Remember that you have God on your side with all his compassion and power.

But just what does this mean? It means that here within you is the same creative Power which built the mind of man, developing it from lower levels until intelligence and imagination were released. Here within you is the love and truth of the creative Spirit of the universe. Here within, if you will only allow it, that individual being which is you can face the world in your own God-given strength and truth. You have just as much of God within you as any other of his creatures. "Fear not, therefore; you are of more value than many sparrows." (Matt. 10:31 R.S.V.) With him you are a majority to meet whatever may come.

He who holds the world within his hand
Will safely hold my heart and understand.

He who keeps the aeons in his power
Will surely guard my heart this troubled hour.

He who owns the farthest realms of space
Can allow my questing life its place.

He who from beginning saw the close
Watches every path my spirit goes.[1]

Today we live in a world haunted by fear. Newspaper, radio, and television bring word of strife, aggression, and revolution. Towering above the confusion is the threat of atomic war. These things from our outer lives impinge on our inner selves. We can allow ourselves to be hedged in by fear until all joy and peace are dimmed in our lives. But this is not meeting the situation with the companionship of God.

These reality-based fears must be faced by a positive and realistic attitude. We must recognize that creative forces for good are active as well as destructive forces. Creation is quieter than destruction. There are human agencies, God-inspired, at work for the education of retarded peoples, for freedom, democracy, and generous co-operation. There are efforts through the United Nations and our own government to meet the threat of war at its source.

[1] Elinor Lennen, "Confidence Against Fear." Used by permission.

We can be alert to the news of these agencies, and lend our voices, our energies, and our means to encourage their work for peace. We can use our influence for faith instead of fear. We can build confidence that God's creative power is available to human minds, and his will can prevail for the future of this troubled world.

O God, there is fear in the world today, fears great and small in every life. Be thou strong within us to comfort and guide, and allay our fears in the light of thy love. AMEN.

24. *Disappointment and Failure*

He shall call upon me, and I will answer him:
I will be with him in trouble.   Ps. 91:15

Disappointment is the common lot. Into every life sooner or later, into most lives often, comes disappointment. Plans are made, perhaps very well made; then something unexpected happens, there is trouble of some kind, and the results are not what we had hoped. There is little to be done, the situation must be accepted as it is.

It has been said that the measure of our maturity is the way in which we meet disappointment. Certainly most adults have learned to "take it in stride" and keep on striding. At least this is the case with the routine disappointments which come in the course of the day or the task. But sometimes a dis-

85

appointment is peculiarly keen, especially when it seems to indicate failure on our own part. It takes courage and character to surmount it and rebuild our morale.

We may take the trouble first of all to the quiet place within, where God waits to restore our confidence. We look at the whole situation in his presence, asking for alertness and insight. For one of the first things we can do with a great disappointment is to *learn* from it. This is the scientist's necessity. Most great scientific achievements are the result of endlessly repeated efforts and painstaking study of efforts which have failed.

Perhaps it is well for us to cultivate a scientific attitude. How was our planning at fault? What were the circumstances we didn't take into account? Did we depend too much on factors unknown to us? How can we change our methods so that we will be more successful another time? Did we rely on others more than was right or needful? Was the failure due to some lack in right relationships?

Another thing we can do with what seems a failure is to make it a means of spiritual growth. Patience is a virtue most of us need to practice. Patience and hope may be cultivated through just beginning again. There must be cheerfulness despite discouragement and faith to seek the way to new planning, always turning inwardly toward the creative Source.

Lord, I have failed. Here are the scattered things,
The plans I made but could not carry through,

The hopes that soared, but fell with broken wings
   To earth again—I bring them all to you.
Take them and me to your creative care
   And use me somehow, Lord. This is my prayer.[1]

When I was much younger I was once responsible for a church project which included planning and working with others over a period of time. Things did not go well, and there were some very discouraging aspects which bowed me down with worry. Then one day I received from a wise older friend some counsel which I have never forgotten and have since passed on to others.

"Remember two things," she said. "First, that you are not responsible for your success; that depends on many circumstances, some of them quite out of your control. You are responsible only for your best and most conscientious efforts. Second, what you see as failure may not be failure in the larger sense. This project is too near you. Try to look upon it not as all-important in itself, but as part of a larger plan, with many elements hidden from your view which may be more important than some which you see. Take the long look, do your best, and leave the rest to God."

After all, failure and success are man-made criteria, and are merely relative. Life moves along with disappointments and triumphs in balance. Every life has its share of both.

Christ met disappointments all along his way. Re-

[1] Grace S. Dawson, "Failure."

87

member how he had to reproach his own intimate friends for their lack of faith, as they disappointed him over and over. "Do you not yet perceive or understand? Are your hearts hardened? Having eyes do you not see, and having ears do you not hear?" (Mark 8:17-18 R.S.V.) Often his plans came to nothing. The people of his hometown grew angry with him and threatened to kill him. (Luke 4:28-29 R.S.V.) In the hour of his greatest need for help and comfort, the three men nearest and dearest to him failed him, and he forgave them, saying, "The spirit indeed is willing, but the flesh is weak" (Mark 14:38 R.S.V.).

And yet—was the life that ended on the cross a failure?

God, be very near to us in the hour of bitter disappointment. Let us not be long cast down, but lift our hearts to a higher level of hope, and use us in thy larger plan. AMEN.

THE
WIDER
VIEW

25. *Seeking the Truth*

And you will know the truth, and the
truth will make you free.
JOHN 8:32 R.S.V.

It is not easy to know the truth. In fact it is most
difficult for anyone to know the whole truth about
any situation, especially one which involves other people with their inner lives. Every person sees things
from an angle peculiarly his own. All his past experience, that which he has known and felt, casts a light
across his mind through which he looks at things. It is
as if he were looking through a lens ground from his
own personal experience, which makes it well nigh
impossible for him to see things exactly as they are.

Especially is this true and especially is it important
in our dealing with other people. It makes it very
hard for those of different background, as the people
of different countries, to find a meeting of minds.
It stands in the way of complete understanding between the generations. Thus it is often hard for

parents to comprehend the attitudes and behavior of their children.

> Never completely whole,
> Oh, never clearly
> Do I discern these passing by.
> Even the soul
> Of him most dearly
> Close to me
> Remains a stranger. For I cannot see
> The world around me save
> Through this intrinsic I,
> A strange, translucent thing,
> Convex, concave,
> Fused in my suffering,
> Marred by fine flaws
> That blur the colors, flex the sight,
> And let me never quite
> See clear, see true,
> Perceive the intimate cause.
>
> And there is little I can do.
> For I must gaze
> "Through a glass darkly" all my days.
> Never shall I behold the clean
> Exquisite outline of the truth until
> Nothing is left between
> And I can look my fill,
> When the last word is spoken,
> And the lens—the lens lies broken.[1]

And yet we want to see the truth. There is great

[1] Grace S. Dawson, "The Lens." Used by permission of *The Saturday Review*.

need in this complicated world of today for clear eyes and minds to face the problems that must be solved. We need objectivity—the ability to approach important questions with open minds, minds seeking the real truth. What can we do to attain this?

One thing we can do, first of all, is to examine and acknowledge our own prejudices. This takes insight and humility. It is not a sign of weakness but of strength and the beginning of wisdom. If we can look into our own past experience and see the underlying situation which produced our feeling, it is the first step toward overcoming an unreasonable attitude in the interests of the truth we seek. If we realize that we have a prejudice to overcome, we are on the way to being clear-minded.

When we are involved with other people, the next step of course is to admit our own prejudice. This takes humility indeed, especially when it is a matter of opposing opinions. But again an acknowledgment of prejudice, with the desire to see all sides and arrive at the truth, will often call forth a like admission from the opposition. The way is cleared for more objective attitudes.

It is clear that he who would know the truth must be humble, ready to put aside notions which will not stand the test of objective reason. He must be willing to wait for the dust of controversy to settle. He must sincerely seek a higher level than partisanship. Christ said, "When he, the Spirit of truth, is come, he will guide you into all truth." (John 16:13.)

In humility we may ask for guidance, and if we

are earnest and patient about the matter, we will often receive real insight, a new understanding which is both broader and deeper. We will ourselves grow, reaching a new height, from which we are able to look over and around our old prejudices, and catch glimpses of the real truth.

O God, who art truth, give us the humility to see our own errors and the patience to wait on thy guidance. Keep us loyal to spiritual truth as far as we can learn to see it. AMEN.

26. *The Wrestling*

Behold, God is great, and we know him not, neither can the number of his years be searched out.
JOB 36:26

Always man has pondered and puzzled about the nature of God. The pagan recognized the powers of nature, feared and sought to placate them. Much later came those studious men who sought to unlock the secrets of the universe, began to discern the patterns and processes of law and order. Science began its work, but the struggle of the mind of man continued. Copernicus and Galileo suffered under the lash of religious authority for their ideas about a sun-centered world system. These ideas have long since been accepted universally and have been expanded into our space-age concepts.

Always poets, students, thinkers, far in advance of
92

the masses, have been misunderstood and often perse-
cuted. Yet slowly, slowly our understanding of the
nature of God's universe and of man himself has been
widened and the frontiers of knowledge have been
pushed back. Like Jacob wrestling with the angel, the
spirit of man has wrestled with the knowledge of
what God's laws demand.

Now we are engaged in a tremendous struggle to
learn another lesson. Two thousand years ago Jesus
hung on a cross for teaching and living the truth that
love is the only truly creative way of life. Today those
who think realize that we are locked in combat with
the forces of evil in man himself, the will-to-power,
the greed, and the brutality which threaten not only his
peace but his very existence. Can we learn in time the
necessity of the law of love as the saving power in this
world of ours?

The spirit, wrestling, cries aloud:

"Who art thou, God? What is thy name?"

> "Lo! I am that which cleaves the cloud
> With tortuous blades of crackling flame.
> Look! I am that which flings the ships
> Storm-twisted on the shuddering land,
> Titanic thunder on my lips,
> Whirlwind and earthquake in my hand.
> Waters and winds, the stars, the sea,
> Hurricane, drouth, the night, the day—
> I am a God too great for thee,
> I am the Law which these obey."

"No! Not too great! Profound, within,
Not to be silenced or denied,
Something there is, has ever been,
Searching thee out, unsatisfied,
Something intrepid, which demands
A sign from thee. *Who art thou, God?*"

> "I am the secret which expands
> The sleeping seed within the clod.
> I am the Life of leaf and root,
> I am the perfect patterning
> That urges to the potential fruit
> Of every crescent, procreant thing.
> I am the throbbing pulse of thee,
> I am the fever in thy blood,
> The subtle beckoning Mystery
> Obeyed but never understood."

"God, thou art more than life alone,
Cells that unite and multiply!
Whence springs the spark that speaks in stone?
Whence leaps the life that dares to die?
Where dost thou hide thee? Why elude
My straining thoughts? *Who art thou, God?*"

> "I am the trouble in thy mood;
> The song that lifts thee from the sod;
> The sacrificial ecstasy
> That sears away thy grosser part;
> I am the Voice that cries to me
> Out of the chaos in thy heart.
> I am thy courage, towering high,
> Beauty and pain and tenderness.

94

Inscrutability am I,
The Riddle that thou canst not guess."

"Oh, God, I will not let thee go
Except thou bless me! Thus I draw
Thy secrets from thee, thus I know
That thou art Truth and Life and Law.
But more thou art—all else above
My heart cries out another name!
God, thou art Love, creative Love,
Forever new and yet the same!
God, thou art Love!" [1]

27. *The World in Travail*

> And he said, "The kingdom of God is as if a
> man should scatter seed upon the ground, and
> should sleep and rise night and day, and the
> seed should sprout and grow, he knows not
> how.   MARK 4:26-27 R.S.V.

Looking out upon the world today we realize
that it is far, far from being the kingdom of God.
Wrong predominates in many places—the rule of
injustice, the prevalence of violence, the presence of
pitiful poverty, ignorance, and hunger. Putting it all
right appears to be only an impossible dream.

Added to this there is the terrible rift in international relationships, the war of ideas rife with
misunderstanding and suspicion. Truth seems no

[1] Grace S. Dawson, "Who Art Thou, God?"

longer evident and clear, but vanishes in a mist of argument, antagonism, prejudices, and downright lies. The very foundations of mutual trust and understanding have been shattered. Is this the world where Christ proposed to build the kingdom of heaven?

Yes, this is the same world. And Christ's way of working has not changed. It is the sowing of the seed, again and again he comes back to that. The seed grows. It grows silently, imperceptibly, we cannot tell how. It is not by wars and victories that the reign of God comes; it is by growth, steady, irresistible, night and day. This is the way we can take part, and this is the way we can tell that the Kingdom is still alive, still advancing.

We crave leadership for our own nation, toward the time when freedom and democracy shall prevail in all the world. But are we sure that in this nation of ours the ideals of freedom and democracy are demonstrated clearly and undeniably? Not until we are living our belief in equal opportunity and justice for all. Not until special privilege is banished and racial discrimination has been wiped from the slate. Not until brotherhood is written more cleanly in our own record can we proclaim it fearlessly to the world at large.

These ideals are in our hearts. The seed has been sown, but it is for us to continue to broadcast it until our own fields are green with growth. Each one of us may look into himself and see whether the seed is growing there. The question probes deep. Am I my brother's keeper right here where I live? Am I living in the Reign of God, now?

The nations have drawn very close together geographically. Thousands of nationals from other countries are living right here in our American cities, walking our streets, attending our schools. Are we bringing them into our homes with friendliness, breaking down barriers of misunderstanding by sharing our way of life? Never was there so much inter-country travel. Never was there such opportunity for friendship between those of different countries. Millions of letters from person to person across national boundaries—these are seeds of the Kingdom. Are we sowing them?

We feel, and rightly, that the government of a democracy is the people. Behind our government is the will, the goodwill of its people. We can let our government feel our desire for international goodwill. The United Nations is not perfect, but it has prevented wars already; it has opened the way to small nations to be heard in the world's councils. Even more, its agencies are promoting the healing of the world's ills, the feeding of the world's hungry, the teaching of the world's ignorant.

Let us know these things, let us promote them. Most of all let us pray for our own personal growth and for the growth of our nation in its leadership. Let us be quick to recognize and support men who raise their voices for right measures and methods, in our own or any other nation. And let us pray that the example of America may be strong and right, and its voice uplifted for the cause of justice and goodwill.

Lord God of Justice, in this stormy hour
  When brutal force pursues a flaunted goal,
Be thou the source of new creative power
  Stirring to birth within our nation's soul.
    Uncloud our vision, keep our purpose clean,
    Gird us with wisdom for the unforeseen.

Lord God of Freedom, on thy name we call,
  Teach us through pain to read thy law aright:
Who would be free must share his good with all,
  Lifting to freedom those of lesser might.
    Silence our clamor, bend our stubborn pride,
    Show us thy dream which will not be denied.

Lord God of Truth, discover to our eyes,
  Here, deep within, thine own most cunning foe.
Unmask our greed and shame our shallow lies,
  Strengthen our wills to do the good we know.
    Lord, as we suffer, grant that in this fire
    We may be tempered unto thy desire.[1]

28. *Immortality*

What is sown is perishable, what is raised
is imperishable. . . . It is sown a physical body,
it is raised a spiritual body.
           I Cor. 15:42, 44 R.S.V.

Life, death, and immortality! These are great concepts, matters for wonder and awe, for long and

---

[1] Grace S. Dawson, "Prayer Out of Conflict."

deep pondering. And mankind has pondered them long. What is the meaning of life; what is it for? Does death draw a final curtain? Is there a going on —an immortality of this personal entity which we call a soul?

This, so they tell me, is the end of all;
This strange deep sleep, those quiet folded hands,
This numbing of the quick and eager mind,
This last slow ebbing of life's fevered sands.
But every fiber of my being cries out
Impassioned protest, and a voice rings clear:
"O cease thy tears! O calm thy troubled heart!
Man in a better life shall reappear.
Fool, to believe that he whose heart was filled
With dreams and visions, he whose shining eyes
Looked to the stars, and even beyond their ken,
Should add but to the dust and never rise" . . .
Life is no futile thing—man is not mocked—
Death means but this, a greater door unlocked.[1]

The human heart rebels at the idea that death puts an end to all the meaning of life. There is too much within us that looks for completion, for fulfillment. The God who has created us to aspire, to look up, to grow and dream would not be a God who would dash such hope to nothing. We must believe that there is an answer to our longing. Our minds tell us that God is reasonable.

And the testimony of science unwittingly bears us out. For science reaffirms what our minds tell us—

[1] Katherine Edelman, "Immortality." Used by permission.

99

that we live in a rational universe where there is an answer to all need, a completed plan in operation, parts that fit together. Evolution itself is witness to an activity which is going somewhere.

Professor Whitehead, one of the wisest philosophers of our generation, basing his ideas soundly on scientific principles, lays emphasis on organism. He sums it up thus:

A thorough-going evolutionary philosophy is inconsistent with materialism. . . . It requires an underlying activity,—expressing itself in individual embodiments, and evolving in achievements of organism. . . . Thus in the process of analyzing the character of nature in itself, we find that the emergence of organism depends on a selective activity which is akin to purpose.[2]

There *is* an underlying activity—God's creative purpose at work. There is purpose in our universe, purpose running through creation, a forward thrust that knows no ending. On every level of evolution this forward-looking pattern appears, in molecule and cell, in the increasing complexity of new forms of life moving always toward greater freedom and wider awareness. Our inner selves, our growing souls long for the greater freedom, the wider knowledge which is still beyond us, as we are limited by the body. We feel that the death of the body could mean the liberation of the soul to new capacities and possibilities.

[2] Alfred North Whitehead, *Science and the Modern World*, p. 157. Used by permission of The Macmillan Company.

In this serene faith the great of all ages have spoken to us. Our poets—Wordsworth, Tennyson, and many others—have borne witness to their belief.

Goethe, the great German writer, once said:

"The thought of death leaves me in perfect peace, for I have a firm conviction that our spirit is a being of indestructible nature: it works on from eternity to eternity: it is like the sun which though it seems to set to our mortal eyes, does not really set but shines on perpetually."

Above all, we have the assurance of Christ himself, whose wisdom made those who heard him marvel. Jesus lived and died in the calm faith of eternal life and eternal values. He said, "God is not the God of the dead, but of the living." (Matt. 22:32.) And after the death of their Lord something happened to his disciples, something so wonderful that it changed them from frightened men to bold soldiers of a new faith. All their doubts vanished, and many things which had been puzzling to them became clear. They went forth to proclaim the gospel of a risen and triumphant Christ.

This we may hold fast, that which is worthy to survive will survive. Ours is the task to choose those ways of living which mean growth—a growth of the spirit which will keep us pointed onward and upward. Ours is the privilege to walk in companionship with the living Christ, so that to us death will be but the opening door to a greater experience.

Give us, O God, a greater vision of the future of

*the soul and a higher resolve in this life of preparation
to rear a structure worthy of perpetuation to thy
glorious eternity.* AMEN.

29. *The Wide Beyond*

> Eye hath not seen, nor ear heard, neither
> have entered into the heart of man, the things
> which God hath prepared for them that love
> him.   I COR. 2:9

We live in a mysterious and marvelous universe.
With all the penetrating research of scientists in this
scientific age we have barely begun to uncover some
of the mystery. With each new discovery the wonder
grows. Scientific theory, which once believed it to be a
mechanical universe, has altered its conception.

"Today," says Sir James Jeans, "the universe begins
to look more like a great thought than like a great
machine." [1]

Through long ages of evolution, the power of God
at work in his creation has developed the intelligence
of man. He has given us the ability to "think some of
his thoughts after him." He has given us the privilege
of pondering the mystery and majesty of his universe.
"How precious also are thy thoughts unto me, O
God! how great is the sum of them!" (Ps. 139:17.)

[1] *The Mysterious Universe*, p. 186. Used by permission of
Cambridge University Press.

Mystery lies all about us in the everyday experiences of nature—the rain, the wind, the sunset—and in the creations of man.

We know that there are sounds beyond our hearing
Around us in the air;
Dog-whistles, radio, night-moths' antennae
Prove they are there.

We know that there are colors past our seeing,
Wider than infra-red,
Wider than ultra-violet—new auroras
And rainbows spread.

Tone-deaf and color-blind—what other senses
Beyond the need of breath
Await us when we pass that glorious hazard
That men call death? [2]

Life itself is a mystery. The scientist in his laboratory has been able to behold the intricate process of cell growth and the production of the new living thing from its parent cells. But the ultimate secret still recedes. No one knows how life originated, nor can anyone fully understand how, without a material agency, the pattern of the mature living creature is passed on from the single cell to the new organism. Yet this mysterious thing happens right around us in all its beautiful complexity.

[2] Dorothy Brown Thompson, "Sensebound." Used by permission.

Earth's crammed with heaven,
And every common bush afire with God;
But only he who sees takes off his shoes,
The rest sit round it and pluck blackberries.[3]

Mind is a mystery. Much knowledge has been accumulated about the nerves and the brain cells and their delicate functioning. But there are areas of action of these minds of ours which seem to pass beyond what is physically possible. Scientists are patiently studying telepathy and extra-sensory perception in the effort to learn more about a realm of experience which has always been a known reality in a world of human beings.

There are dreams and visions, bringing knowledge of faraway people or of future events. Thousands of such experiences, well authenticated, are in the records of the Society for Psychical Research of both Great Britain and America. These things cannot be explained by any scientific knowledge which we now have. Shall we know sometime? Or are these things part of the mystery which will be unveiled only after we have crossed the barrier of death and reached some higher state?

Here lies the greatest mystery of all—what is the nature of that region which lies beyond this life, "the undiscover'd country, from whose bourne no traveller returns"? We cannot know, but perhaps it is good sometimes to wonder and muse. Here and now life denotes growth; while we are living we are

---

[3] Elizabeth Barrett Browning, from "Aurora Leigh."

learning and our knowledge grows with experience. If the life of the spirit continues after the body is left behind, does growth continue also? Do the spirits which have passed on, with the wider awareness of a higher spiritual level continue to learn?

Do they still feel an interest in this planet with its poignant problems? Do they perhaps work in groups with a greater love and understanding than that known on this earth plane and share our trials and help toward solutions? What lies over the border in the wide beyond?

O God, help us to see heaven in all around us, the spiritual robed in the material. Keep our hearts open to wonder, and give us a serene faith in thy mysterious purpose for thy creation. AMEN.

30. *The Eternal Beauty*

O worship the Lord in the beauty of holiness.
Ps. 96:9

Deep within each one of us the creator God has placed a love of beauty. In all that we make or do we feel it important that the result should be as beautiful as possible. Beauty is very close to creativity itself. From earliest times men added to their work that which gave it beauty—carving the tools, weaving the fabrics, shaping and painting the clay utensils to forms which pleased them. Beauty was and is a significant part of life. Out of man's love for beauty has arisen the whole world of art—music, poetry, painting, drama.

But what, then, *is* beauty? This is a large question and it has no simple answer. But one thing we know: Beauty affords us a deep inner satisfaction of a certain kind, and the things we call beautiful are those which give us this satisfaction. It is the satisfaction of a real hunger, and one of the things for which we hunger is wholeness or completeness.

Beautiful things are complete things; they have design or pattern. In forming the design the artist—painter, composer, poet—gathers together what is needed for completeness and discards irrelevant material. The finished work must be a rounded and complete whole.

It is this completeness which satisfies us. So much of life is broken and fragmentary, partial experiences which seem to have no relationship with the rest of life. This is no doubt why we find joy and a sense of peace in a thing of beauty like a great cathedral or the Sistine "Madonna" or a Beethoven sonata. Every part is related to every other part, and the whole is completed, its full self.

Look now at the beauty of the universe around us, the work of the supreme Intelligence, the consummate Artist. Design permeates everything. The very building blocks of creation, the atoms, are perfect in design. Each has its proper number of electrons circling in their orbits around the central nucleus, as the planets circle the sun, making possible infinite combinations, making possible life itself.

Moving from level to level of evolving creation we find the same perfection of design—the exquisite architecture of the crystal, the marvelous patterning of the snowflake, the intricate structure of the cell with its pattern of mystery in reproducing itself. Consider the design of a flower—petal, stamen, and seed-bearing ovary—unique and complete. Consider the vast number of animal forms, each complete in function, and each revealing its own special beauty.

O worship the Lord in the beauty of *wholeness*. For this is the same word as holiness. The holiness of God is proclaimed in the wholeness of his creation. He is the supreme Artist, and he will not betray his artistry. Yes, there is a message to the soul, a message reiterated in all that lies around us. There is a great design; there is an underlying purpose which goes steadily on to fulfillment.

God is One; and the universe is his, a whole completing itself. We who are in the midst of the pattern cannot see its completion, but God has made it plain. He has set it in parables to teach us. Life wakens to new life—the egg to the birdling, the seed to the new plant, the caterpillar to the butterfly. Death is not the end; it is only the close of one chapter. There is an answer to the longing for the life beyond; there is a gathering together of the uncompleted fragments to new opportunity. There is a new level of emergence; the spirit has its intuitive knowledge and awaits its new birth.

The days blow by like winds, and every gust
    Scatters the dust
Of all we were and all we had to say
    Widely away.
Therefore, when this frail structure known as I
    Quiet shall lie
Beneath the drifting fragrance of new bloom
    In some calm room,
I have for clear indelible utterance
    But one brief chance,
While little, brittle memories of me
    Rise suddenly,
While death's imperious dignity and pride
    Have magnified
My small import to those who gather there
    To weep, or stare.

Then let my silence cry, " I have gone out
    Through dusk and doubt
And all these trivial barriers to the place
    Of light and space,
Where God's winds blow from burning star to star,
    Where God's thoughts are.
I do not sleep, nothing can fetter me,
    I have gone free
To follow Beauty to her Fountainhead.
    I am not dead." [1]

---

[1] Grace S. Dawson, "Consummation." Used by permission of *Star-News,* Pasadena, California.

FOR FURTHER READING

The list below is by no means intended to be comprehensive. It includes merely in each category a few suggested titles which I have personally found most helpful.

For Bible Study

Barclay, William. "Daily Study Bible Series." Philadelphia: The Westminster Press. Fourteen in the series have been published to date.

The Interpreter's Bible. 12 vols. Nashville: Abingdon Press, 1952-57. Vols. VII and VIII.

The Way of Prayer

Day, Albert E. *An Autobiography of Prayer.* New York: Harper & Row, Publishers, Inc., 1952.

Magee, John. *Reality and Prayer.* New York: Harper & Row, Publishers, Inc., 1957.

Radcliffe, Lynn J. *Making Prayer Real.* Apex edition. Nashville: Abingdon Press, 1961.

Steere, Douglas C. *On Beginning from Within.* New York: Harper & Brothers, 1943.

Wyon, Olive. *The School of Prayer.* 7th edition. Naperville, Ill.: Alec R. Allenson, Inc., 1958.

For Daily Inspiration

Kelly, Thomas R. *A Testament of Devotion*. New York: Harper & Row, Publishers, Inc., 1941.

Miller, Samuel. *The Life of the Soul*. New York: Harper & Row, Publishers, Inc., 1951.

Strong, Mary, editor. *Letters from the Scattered Brotherhood*. New York: Harper & Row, Publishers, Inc., 1948.

Tourville, Abbe de. *Letters of Direction*. New York: Thomas Y. Crowell Company, 1939.

Underhill, Evelyn. *Fruits of the Spirit, Light of Christ, and Abba: Meditations Based on the Lord's Prayer*. London: Longmans, Green & Co., 1956.

Daily Prayers

Baillie, John. *A Diary of Private Prayer*. New York: Charles Scribner's Sons, 1949.

Miller, Samuel. *Prayers for Daily Use*. New York: Harper & Row, Publishers, Inc., 1957.

INDEX TO POETRY

111

112